Covenant
Claiming your Covenant Citizenship Benefits and Inheritance

There Are Many Benefits Listed within the Covenant that will Enable Us to Live a Victorious Life as A Christian

By
Pastor James L. Monteria

Come and Learn of Me Ministries, Int'l
P.O. Box 932
Chesterfield, VA 23832

Covenant
Claiming your Covenant Citizenship Benefits and Inheritance

Unless otherwise indicated, all Scriptures are taken from the King James Version of the Bible

ISBN 978-0-9897704-3-9

Copyright © 2011 by CLM Ministries

Published by CLM Publishing
P.O. Box 932
Chesterfield, VA 23832

Printed in the United States of America; All rights reserved under International Copyright Law. Contents and cover may not be reproduced in whole or in part in any form without the expressed written consent of the publisher.

Table of CONTENTS

Section I

I What is a Covenant?	Page 1
II Biblical Covenant	Page 5
A) God's covenant "Noah"	Page 5
B) God's covenant "Abraham"	Page 5
C) God's covenant "Moses"	Page 6
D) God's covenant "David"	Page 7
E) New Covenant "Jesus"	Page 7
F) Marriage covenant	Page 9
Roles of Husband & Wife	Page 10
G) Old Covenant Vs. New Covenant	Page 12

Section II

Claiming your Covenant Citizenship Benefits	Page 17
1) The Constitution	Page 23
2) Government Assistance	Page 26
3) Access to Almighty God	Page 29
4) Peace of God	Page 32
5) Presence of God	Page 35
6) Authority	Page 38
7) Healing	Page 41
8) Power	Page 43
9) Anointing	Page 46
10) Divine Protection	Page 49
11) Revelation	Page 52

Section III

The Nature of a Covenant	Page 55
A Continuation of claiming your Covenant Citizenship Benefits	
12) Mercy	Page 62
13) Faith	Page 65
14) Liberty	Page 68
15) Joy	Page 71
16) Military Might	Page 74
17) Stability	Page 77
18) Global Family	Page 80

Section IV
    Possessing Our Inheritance   Page 84
    Law of Faith   Page 99
    Law of Confession   Page 108

Section V
    Daily Favor Confession   Page 123
    Faith Declaration (Who I am)   Page 124
    Monday – I walk in Love and faith   Page 124
    Tuesday – I guidance of the Holy Spirit   Page 126
    Wednesday – Walking the power of God   Page 127
    Thursday – I am healed   Page 128
    Friday – All my needs are provided   Page 129
    Saturday – Favor and Wisdom   Page 130
    Sunday – I walk in the Blessing   Page 131

Covenant Decision   Page 134
About the Author   Page 136

Remember
You can't claim what you don't know

Hosea 4:6 *says "my people are destroyed for lack of knowledge. Because they reject knowledge…"*

"Knowledge of your Covenant Benefits and Inheritance"

Acknowledgement

First and foremost, I would not even know God, or be able to write anything about Him, were it not for His grace and mercy! I have come to appreciate the grace of God, the Lordship of Jesus Christ, and the Holy Spirit's presence in my life and my ministry, even more than words could express.

Section I

What is a Covenant?

What is a Covenant?

The purpose of this book is to help understand "What is a Covenant", and what has been provided for us through the covenant as a result of being baptized into the body of Christ, and to show the significance of our relationship with Almighty God.

Hebrews 5:9 "and being made perfect, he became the author of eternal salvation unto all them that obey him;"

Hebrews 8:6 "but now hath he obtained a more excellent ministry, by how much also he is the mediator of a better covenant, which was established upon better promises."

Hebrews 9:16-17 "For where a testament is, there must also of necessity be the death of the testator. [17]For a testament is of force after men are dead: otherwise it is of no strength at all while the testator liveth."

Our focus in this book will be primarily on the biblical covenant and the scriptural understanding. I sense that the time in which we live it is imperative that we know who we are, what we have, and what we can do.

It is all tied to our understanding of the covenant and our benefits as citizens in the Kingdom of God. We will cover the aspect of a nature covenant in Section II. The word covenant occurs 280 times in the Old Testament and 33 times in the New Testament; in its most basic form, every covenant takes the form of God commanding, "I will be their God, and they will be my people." (Jeremiah 31:33c) and then stipulating the terms of the relationship.

In its details, a covenant describes the way in which God expects man to behave, the rewards that he will receive for obedience and the punishments he will endure for disobedience.

There are two basic words in Scripture for covenant. The Hebrew word, used in the Old Testament is **b'rit (or) b'rith (280 times)**, means **"to bind." It is a binding agreement between two parties.**

This Hebrew word occurs in the name of the well-known Jewish organization B'nai B'rith, which means, literally, *"Sons of Covenant."*

The Greek word used in the New Testament, is **diatheke (33 times),** and this means **"to set something out in order."** It suggests the setting forth of specific terms and conditions.

Each of these words - diatheke in Greek and b'rit in Hebrews is regular translated by two different English words: covenant and testament. The English word used in each case varies according to the context.

In English, we do not normally think of covenant and testament as being the same. We limit the word testament to a legal document that, as scripture points out, comes into force only after the death of the one who made the testament. (Hebrews 9:16-17).

On the other hand, we do not usually think of a covenant as being necessarily associated with death, the death of the parties to the covenant.

Another thing, as we understand the Word of God accurately we will discover that covenants fall into two classes:

CONDITIONAL - A covenant which guarantees that God will do His part when the human requirements stipulated in that covenant are met.

UNCONDITIONAL - Distinguished from a conditional covenant by the fact that its ultimate fulfillment is promised by God and depends upon God's power and sovereignty for its fulfillment.

The conditions and stipulations of the covenant are dictated and imposed by God and man has no ability to negotiate the terms.

Biblical Covenants

In the Bible God made Covenants with people regarding salvation, and the **Old Testament Covenant** revolved around salvation through the Laws of Moses. **The New Testament covenant** promises salvation through belief in Jesus Christ as Savior. Both covenants gave us the opportunity to be forgiven for our sins. Understanding the covenants gives us a better understanding of God and the sacrifice made for us by Christ.

A). God's covenant with Noah

Genesis 9:1-18; (unconditional) - One of God's first Covenants with people were given to Noah. God re-established the earth with Noah and promised never again to destroy it with a flood. "And I will establish my covenant with you; neither shall all flesh be cut off any more by the waters of a flood; neither shall there anymore be a flood to destroy the earth." (Genesis 9:11).

Noah's Ark was an early foreshadowing of the plan of salvation that God had in store for us with Jesus Christ. Those that took refuge in the ark were saved, just as those of us who take refuge in Christ are saved.

B). God's covenant with Abraham

(Genesis 12:1-4; 13:14-17; 15:1-7; 17:1-8 ;) (Unconditional) To establish His people, "And he brought him forth abroad, and said, look now toward heaven, and tell the stars, if thou be able to number them: and he said unto him, so shall thy seed be." (Genesis 15:5) Because of his faith, Abraham was made the father of the nation of Israel.

Because of his faith, Abraham was made the father of the nation of Israel. God promised, through Abraham, a homeland for His people: "And I will give unto thee, and to thy seed after thee, the land wherein thou art a stranger, all the land of Canaan, for an **everlasting possession**; and I will be their God." (Genesis 17:8)

C). God's covenant with Moses

Exodus 20:1–31:18; (conditional) At Sinai, God established His covenant with His people through Moses. "For thou art and holy people unto the LORD thy God:

The LORD thy God hath chosen thee to be a special people unto himself, above all people that are upon the face of the earth." (Deuteronomy 7:6).

God presented Moses with the Law and promised His people salvation through the faithful keeping of the Law. "Know therefore that the LORD thy God, He is God, the faithful God, which keepeth covenant and mercy with them that love him and keep his commandments to a thousand generations;" (Deuteronomy 7:9)

Though the Law was a path to salvation, it was also a curse and a burden. Continual sacrifices had to be made to wash away sin and stringent standards of living must be obeyed to remain clean. Later, the covenant of Christ would free us from the curse of the Law because Christ made Himself the final and perfect sacrifice.

D). God's covenant with David

2 Samuel -7:416; 1 Chronicles 17:3-15; (Unconditional) He promised salvation and then with David God promised the coming Messiah.

"Howbeit the LORD would not destroy the house of David, because of the covenant that he had made with David, and as he promised to give a light to him and to his sons forever." (2 Chronicles 21:7)

The New Covenant establishes the Law in our hearts. "But this shall be the covenant that I will make with the house of Israel; after those days, saith the LORD, I will put my law in their inward parts, and write it in their hearts; and will be their God, and they shall be my people." (Jeremiah 31:33)

The sacrifice of Christ, no other sacrifice must be made. We must only believe in His saving sacrifice and internalize the Law by allowing the Holy Spirit to dwell in us.

E). New Covenant - Jesus the Messiah

(Jeremiah 31:31-40; Unconditional) The New Promise is fulfilled in the Messiah. "Behold, I will send my messenger, and he shall prepare the way before me: and the Lord, whom ye seek, shall suddenly come to his temple, even the messenger of the covenant, whom ye delight in: behold, he shall come, saith the LORD of hosts." (Malachi 3:1)

It was put into effect by Jesus' death. "And for this cause he is the mediator of the New Testament that by means of death, for the redemption of the transgressions that were under the first testament, they which are called might receive the promise of eternal inheritance."

(Hebrews 9:15) And it was sealed with Christ's blood. "Likewise also the cup after supper, saying, and this cup is the New Testament in my blood, which is shed for you." (Luke 22:20)

God's New Covenant with His people is superior to the old because it offers complete forgiveness.

"There is therefore now no condemnation to them which are in Christ Jesus, who walk not after the flesh, but after the Spirit." (Romans 8:1)

Jesus' final sacrifice offers us freedom from the law "Christ hath redeemed us from the curse of the law, being made a curse for us:" (Galatians 3:13a)

Jesus ministry is superior to the ministry of the Law because His sacrifice ended the need for blood sacrifice and established the New Covenant of salvation through faith in Him.

"But now hath he obtained a more excellent ministry, by how much also he is the mediator of a better covenant, which was established upon better promises." (Hebrews 8:6)

Only the sacrifice of Christ could have completed the Law: "How much more shall the blood of Christ, who through the eternal Spirit offered himself without spot to God, purge your conscience from dead works to serve the living God?" (Hebrews 9:14)

Christ gave Himself perfect, without sin, to free us from the death penalty of sin. By His perfect sacrifice we are set free.

Since the beginning of time, God has wanted to have a relationship with us and has provided us with a way of communing with Him after the fall from grace, when sin entered the world and separated us from God, but in His mercy He has provided us with opportunities for restoration.

Through Noah, Abraham, Moses and David, God established His Old Covenant of salvation. Through Christ, He perfected His covenant with us and inscribed it on our hearts with the indwelling of His Holy Spirit. He taught us to appreciate sacrifice with the Old Covenant and provided us with the perfect sacrifice with Christ. His covenants are kept and we, through His grace, are saved by them.

F). Marriage Covenant (Genesis 2:21-25)

A marriage agreement is not only a covenant between man and wife, but the name and blessing of God are often invoked as well. The marriage union is the closest relationship between two human beings. When a man and women decide to join together in marriage, they should do so with full realization of their responsibilities.

Marriage is serious business. As they pronounce the marriage vows in faith, the power of God goes into operation and a miracle takes place.

They are united by God and become as one in His sight. Their union is threefold: They are joined together spiritually by God, legally by contract and physically when the marriage is consummated. A husband and wife are joined together as Jesus is joined to the church. It is a miraculous union.

The state enters into marriage covenants because it licenses marriage, and the families involved usually pledge to work together to strengthen the marriage bond between man and wife. Marriage is the oldest institution in the world, honored in the OT and the NT and approved by God.

The marriage covenant is not merely sacred in its own right. It is sacred also because it typifies other relationships of great spiritual significance. The first and the most important of these is the relationship that God desires to have with His people.

In Hosea, as in Jeremiah, there is a prophetic promise that God will eventually bring Israel back into covenant with Himself and thereby restore His relationship to them as their Husband. God declared the following:

It will come about in that day," declares the LORD, "That you will call Me Ishi [**my Husband**] And will no longer call Me Baali [**my Master**] Hosea 2:16 (NAS)

Then, Hosea 2:18, God spoke of a new covenant that He would make with them. In verse 19 and 20, He pictured the result of this covenant as the restoration of His marriage relationship to them:

"Will betroth you to Me forever; Yes, I will betroth you to Me in righteousness and in justice, in loving-kindness and in compassion, 20And I will betroth you to Me in faithfulness. Then you will know the LORD. (Hosea 2:19-20)"

Basic roles of Husband and wife:
The Husband contribution:

Please see 1 Corinthians 11:7, Ephesians 5:22-31, and Hebrews 13:4);

All of the covenants between God and Man in the Bible are really based on our Creator's unmerited favor and loving kindness towards His fallen and sinful creatures.

Although man's expected response to God's grace may be stated differently in one covenant as compared to another, God always meets man on the basis of grace. Man's proper response is always to come from the heart resulting in repentance, cleansing, a renewed spirit and worship as stated beautifully in Psalm 51.

The Wife's contribution:

Please see (Proverbs 31:10-31).

Man may choose to live in covenant relationship (faithfulness) and redeem the promises of God, or may choose to disregard his obligations and accept the consequences, but that is all the freedom that man has in the relationship.

God may supersede the covenant or may subsequently reveal additional details of the covenant, but it cannot be altered by man, nor will God alter it after it has been established.

G). Old Covenant and New Covenant Compared and Contrasted

Now the first covenant had regulations for worship and an earthly sanctuary. For a tent was prepared, the outer one, in which were the lamp stand and the table and the bread of the Presence; it is called the Holy Place.

Behind the second curtain stood a tent called the Holy of Holies, having the golden altar of incense and the ark of the covenant covered on all sides with gold, which contained a golden urn holding the manna, and Aaron's rod that budded, and the tables of the covenant; above it were the cherubim of Glory overshadowing the Mercy Seat. Of these things we cannot now speak in detail.

These preparations having thus been made, the priests go continually into the outer tent, performing their ritual duties; but into the second only the high priest goes, and he but once a year, and not without taking blood which he offers for himself and for the errors of the people.

By this the Holy Spirit indicates that the way into the sanctuary is not yet opened as long as the outer tent is still standing (which is symbolic for the present age).

According to this arrangement, gifts and sacrifices are offered which cannot perfect the conscience of the worshiper, but deal only with food and drink and various ablutions, regulations for the body imposed until the time of reformation.

When Christ appeared as a high priest of the good things that have come, then through the greater and more perfect tent (not made with hands, that is, not of this creation) he entered once for all into the Holy Place, taking not the blood of goats and calves but his own blood, thus securing an eternal redemption. For if the sprinkling of defiled persons with the blood of goats and bulls and with the ashes of a heifer sanctifies for the purification of the flesh, how much more shall the blood of Christ, who through the eternal Spirit offered himself without blemish to God, purify your conscience from dead works to serve the living God.

Therefore He [Jesus] is the mediator of a new covenant, so that those who are called may receive the promised eternal inheritance, since a death has occurred which redeems them from the transgressions under the first covenant.

For where a will is involved, the death of the one who made it must be established. For a will takes effect only at death, since it is not in force as long as the one who made it is alive. Hence even the first covenant was not ratified without blood.

When every commandment of the law had been declared by Moses to all the people, he took the blood of calves and goats, with water and scarlet wool and hyssop, and sprinkled the book itself and all the people, saying, "This is the blood of the covenant which God commanded you." And in the same way he sprinkled with the blood both the tent and all the vessels used in worship. Indeed, under the law almost everything is purified with blood, and without the shedding of blood there is no forgiveness of sins.

Thus it was necessary for the copies of the heavenly things to be purified with these rites, but the heavenly things themselves with better sacrifices than these.

For Christ has entered, not into a sanctuary made with hands, a copy of the true one, but into heaven itself, now to appear in the presence of God on our behalf. Nor was it to offer himself repeatedly, as the high priest enters the Holy Place yearly with blood not his own; for then he would have had to suffer repeatedly since the foundation of the world. But as it is, he has appeared once for all at the end of the age to put away sin by the sacrifice of himself.

Just as it is appointed for men to die once, and after that comes judgment, so Christ, having been offered once to bear the sins of many, will appear a second time, not to deal with sin but to save those who are eagerly waiting for him. (Hebrews 9)

Are we beginning to commend ourselves again? Or do we need, as some do, letters of recommendation to you, or from you? You yourselves are our letter of recommendation, written on your hearts, to be known and read by all men; and you show that you are a letter from Christ delivered by us, written not with ink but with the Spirit of the Living God, not on tablets of stone but on tablets of human hearts. Such is the confidence that we have through Christ toward God. Not that we are competent of ourselves to claim anything as coming from us; our competence is from God, who has made us competent to be ministers of a new covenant, not in a written code but in the Spirit; for the written code kills, but the Spirit gives life.

Now if the dispensation of death, carved in letters on stone, came with such splendor that the Israelites could not look at Moses' face because of its brightness, fading as this was, will not the dispensation of the Spirit be attended with greater splendor?

For if there was splendor in the dispensation of condemnation, the dispensation of righteousness must far exceed it in splendor. Indeed, in this case, what once had splendor has come to have no splendor at all, because of the splendor that surpasses it. For if what faded away came with splendor, what is permanent must have much more splendor. Since we have such a hope, we are very bold, not like Moses, who put a veil over his face so that the Israelites might not see the end of the fading splendor.

But their minds were hardened; for to this day, when they read the old covenant, that same veil remains, because only through Christ is it taken away. Yes, to this day whenever Moses is read a veil lies over their minds; but when a man turns to the Lord the veil is removed.

Now the Lord is the Spirit, and where the Spirit of the Lord is, there is freedom. And we all, with unveiled face, beholding the glory of the Lord, are being changed into his likeness from one degree of glory to another; for this comes from the Lord who is the Spirit." (2 Corinthians 3)

Summary

The Bible is the story of God's covenantal kingdom – its creation, its corruption by sin and folly, and God's gracious redemption of that kingdom to the praise of the glory of His grace. The central theme of the Bible, the covenantal kingdom of God, reveals the nature of the Triune God as a God of love who has called man into a fellowship of love with Himself.

Claiming your Covenant Citizenship Benefits

If you had just become a citizen of the United States, wouldn't you want to know what benefits you have inherent with your new citizenship? You would want to know the benefits, the rights, the freedoms, and etc. that are guaranteed to you by our Constitution.

Unfortunately, however, many United States citizens live beneath their means and their rightful status because of their ignorance of their benefits. Even worse are those that know about the benefits, but are too lazy to operate on their knowledge and stake a claim to what is rightfully theirs.

Knowledge is good to combat the ignorance, but after receiving the information concerning the benefits, the citizens must have the desire to act upon that information to bring about a change in their lives.

Likewise, in the body of Christ, we are born-again into the Kingdom of God and become Kingdom citizens. God Word says "my people are destroyed for lack of knowledge or because they reject knowledge". Hosea 4:6

God's Riches!

Romans 10:12 states "For there is no distinction between Jew and Greek, for the same Lord over all is rich to all who call upon Him."

Paul wanted the Romans to have a better understanding about God's nature. Specifically, he wanted them to understand that God abounds in riches.

This means that God does not lack anything. He has an abundance of everything—wisdom, power, resources, talent, abilities, gifts, and every other form of riches we can imagine!

What kinds of riches is the Bible talking about? First, there are spiritual riches—salvation, peace, eternal life, forgiveness of sins, authority over demonic forces, healing, full access to His presence, and all of the fruit and gifts of the Holy Spirit! What more could we ask for? But there is even more! He is ready to meet ALL of our needs—financial, emotional, mental, and practical.

We must combat ignorance to the Word and to God's promises through worship services, bible studies, ministries such as this one, and other bible teaching tools.

Even after you hear the truth of the Word of God, you must make the decision to stake a claim on the benefits of your new citizenship as we are encouraged to do in James 1:22.

As the saying goes," The Word of God will work if you work it."

These lessons are designed to teach you some of your new benefits, but you must apply the teachings to your life if you are ever going to receive anything from them.

Claim your benefits and prosper! God is not stingy with these riches, but we must learn how to acquire them. He gives *RICHES* "TO ALL WHO CALL UPON HIM." We access all of these riches by calling on Him and applying His principles.

For example, He promises that we will *reap what we sow*. This means we need to be faithful in sowing the things God has given us. As we call on Him and sow seeds from our resources, we can expect that He will meet our needs and reward us with His riches.

Today, all of God's riches are available to you, and He wants you to have them. Call on Him. Turn to Him. Seek Him. Make sure you are sowing seeds with your time, talent, and treasure.

Be faithful with what God has given you. Moreover, do not limit Him! He can do above and beyond all you can expect or think.

Fulfilling the Requirement

Many give their lives to Christ, but never learn how to live a victorious life in Christ. This is why I get up so early every morning and seek God for a message to share with you. It is my ministry to help you to attain the biblical information you need to grow and live victoriously in Christ.

Hosea 4:6a; "My people are destroyed for lack of knowledge… "

We have some key benefits of being a citizen of the Kingdom of God. As you have noticed there is a requirement in the process. Citizenship does not guarantee receipt of the benefits. Receiving the benefits is a threefold process: Information, Request and Application.

Let's see how these things apply to our lives today:

Knowledge: Hosea said that God's people are destroyed for the lack of knowledge. Simply put, you cannot apply what you do not know. There are millions of citizens of the United States that are ignorant of their benefits. If they never learn about the benefits, they will never enjoy them.

These citizens will not make maximum use of their citizenship because of their lack of knowledge. It is the same way in the Kingdom of God. As I previously stated, many give their lives to Christ, but never learn how to live a victorious life in Christ. If we follow the pattern of Jesus, we will rise early every morning and seek God for His wisdom and understanding of God Himself and His ways, His Kingdom, Our Lord and Saviour Jesus who is the Christ, and the Holy Spirit. This will help us to attain the biblical information we need to grow and live victoriously in Christ.

Petitions: If I were to hold a seminar on the benefits of U.S. citizenship with a 1,000 citizens and detail clearly how they can maximize their benefits by simply going down to a local government office. Then filling out a few forms, invariably, many would simply be too lazy to go down to the office and fill out the forms, making their request known.

In Christ, there are no forms and there are no offices. As born-again believers, we have the right to come to the Father, in the Name of the Jesus, and make our request known unto God; staking a claim on our benefits. After we receive the information about our rights, privileges, and benefits, we still need to make the request.

Petitions: Then there are those that learn about their benefits, fill out the request, receive what they asked for; but then don't actually use what they receive for their good. Let's say that I offered umbrellas to everyone. You then take me up on my offer and ask for the umbrella. I reach into my storehouse and give you an umbrella to help you make it through rough weather unchanged.

Now the onus is on you to use it. I did everything I could for you, but you still need to apply that umbrella to your situation, if you are going to walk through the storm unchanged.

That's how it is with God. You receive these messages about your benefits (information), you make the confession at the end of the message (request) and God blesses you to receive what you have asked for; now it is up to you to apply what He gives you and actually maximize it in your life.

Don't enjoy it for a week and then put it away. Like that umbrella, you need to know where it is, when the time comes to use it.

Do you know your benefits?

Great, then you have information. Have you claimed your benefits? Great, then you have made the request. But have you applied what you have received? A petition brings about liberation! We will only prosper in accordance with what we apply!

I want to encourage you not only to know your benefits, rights, privileges as a child of God, but claim them and walk in them on a daily basis.

Psalm 103:1-5, says…"forget not all his benefits: ¹Bless the LORD, O my soul: and all that is within me, bless his holy name. ²Bless the LORD, O my soul, and forget not all his benefits: ³Who forgiveth all thine iniquities; who healeth all thy diseases; ⁴Who redeemeth thy life from destruction; who crowneth thee with lovingkindness and tender mercies; ⁵Who satisfieth thy mouth with good things; so that thy youth is renewed like the eagle's."

1. THE CONSTITUTION

II Timothy 2:15 "Study to shew thyself approved unto God, a workman that needeth not to be ashamed, rightly dividing the word of truth"

The Constitution! The United States is still the symbol of hope for most of the world. Many people come to the United States after having dreamed of it all their lives. They finally get here and work hard to make a better life for themselves and for their family. At some point, they might be afforded the opportunity to join this country (by oath) as a citizen.

When they do, they do it to receive and retain all the rights and benefits inherent to citizenship. The problem is that most don't really understand their benefits, nor truly understand their rights. We have many rights and the base document for those rights is our Constitution. Now, let's be honest, how many people have read through and understand the Constitution? Not many.

Not only that, many don't even know where to go to find a copy of it. You can't read what you can't find. Likewise, Christianity is a symbol of hope for a dying and decaying world. Many people come to Christ for a better life for themselves and for their family.

They are afforded the opportunity to become a citizen of the Kingdom of God (by oath) and -- praise God -- many do so daily; by repenting of their sins and accepting Jesus Christ as their Lord.

Now, after they are born-again and are citizens of the Kingdom, they, too, have many rights and privileges inherent to this new citizenship.

Our base document is also our Constitution (the Bible). The big difference is that most born-again believers today, unlike the believers in the Old Testament, have free access to our Constitution.

We have copies of it on our coffee table, in our car, on the internet, at church, etc. Now how foolish would it be to become a citizen of a new kingdom and carry around a copy of the Constitution with you all the time and never read it?

Summary:

1. Jesus came to re-establish the Kingdom of God in the earth.
2. We are born again into His Kingdom.
3. His Kingdom has a Constitution that outlines our rights and benefits.
4. Our King has ensured that we have free access to our Constitution.
5. It is our responsibly to read it and clearly understand the rights and privileges to its promises.
6. Our text teaches us that as citizens of this new Kingdom, part of our responsibility is to study the Constitution.

7. Citizens who ignore the Constitution are still citizens, but their ignorance limits them from enjoying the full benefits of their citizenship. Do you have a copy of our Constitution, the Bible? When was the last time you read it?

CONFESSION

Heavenly Father, I am a born-again believer. I have declared my citizenship in Your Kingdom. I have a copy of the Constitution and I declare that I will read it, study it, apply it, and receive from it. I can have what it says I can have. I can do what it says I can do. I can be what it says I can be. I will never, ever be the same. In Jesus' name Amen!

2. HEAVENLY GOVERNMENT ASSISTANCE

Philippians 4:19 (AMP) "And my God will liberally supply (fill to the full) your every need according to His riches in glory in Christ Jesus."

Government Assistance! The United States is still the symbol of hope for most of the world. Many people come to the United States by any and all possible means. By the time they get here, the few resources they had are depleted and they set out to reestablish their lives in this new country. Because of their situation, many are forced to receive government assistance for their financial and medical well-being. This system is designed to help those that cannot help themselves and help them get to a point where they can.

When we repent of our sin and are born-again into the Kingdom of God, we are made citizens of heaven. With this new citizenship comes the right to Godly Government Assistance. There are some differences, however, between the assistance the United States provides and the assistance of God.

Summary:

1. The Resources: Although the United States is a global super power and a great nation, we are a nation in debt and our national deficit is reaching never before seen levels. The resources of our nation, although plenteous, have their limits. The resources in the Kingdom of God are limitless. The only limits that God seemingly has are the limits that we place on Him. He has no boundaries and His resources have no limits. He owns the cattle on a thousand hills **(Ps 50:10)**! Our text tells us that He has riches in glory in Christ Jesus!

2. The Time Frame: The U.S. wants people to be able to get off of assistance as soon as possible and to be able to make it on their own. There have been changes in recent years to limit the time frame of assistance and to make sure that this process is carried out. On the contrary, in the Kingdom of God, God wants us to receive His assistance and to depend on Him for the rest of our lives!

3. The Scope: U.S. Government assistance is mainly limited to food and health care. There are other systems in place, but those two are the primary means of assistance.

On the contrary, in the Kingdom of God, we have access to whatever the NEED is that presents itself in our lives. Our text tells us that God will liberally supply (fill to the full) our every need. If there is a need for food, He can supply it. If there is a need for healing, He can supply it.

If there is a need for peace, He can supply it. If there is a need for protection, He can do that, too. And the list can go on. Be careful, however, to understand that the text promises that our Godly Kingdom will provide all our NEED; the Apostle Paul did not say our every WANT. God is not a genie in a bottle waiting for us to make wishes, but He is a Loving, Caring, Compassionate, and Limitless King; ready to meet the needs of His people.

Question: If it is Monday morning, what do you NEED to make it through this week? Don't try to make it on your own. If you are a citizen of heaven, then stake a claim on your Godly Government Assistance. The Holy Spirit will assist you to overcome every obstacle and reach every goal!

CONFESSION

Heavenly Father, I am a born-again believer. I have declared my citizenship in Your Kingdom. I have a right to your assistance. I stake a claim on your limitless resources and declare that all my needs are met according to your riches in glory. Whatever the need, you are the supply. I receive the supply and enjoy my Godly benefits. In Jesus' Name Amen

3. ACCESS TO HEAVENLY FATHER

Matthews 27:50, 51, "And Jesus gave another loud cry, and gave up his spirit. And the curtain of the Temple was parted in two from end to end; and there was an earth-shock; and the rocks were broken."

No other human being before or after Jesus could ever compare with Him. He was born like no one else was ever born, lived like no one else ever lived, suffered the greatest penalty for something He did not do, and experienced the greatest event ever documented in history.

The Resurrection from the Dead! Yes, Jesus was the greatest, but He also came so that we could operate in His greatness (John 10:10). His death, burial, and resurrection bridged the gap between fallen man and a Holy God. Jesus' sacrifice allows us the opportunity to be born-again (John 3:3) and to receive a new citizenship in His Kingdom.

We now belong to a new Kingdom, with new laws and new benefits. To fully understand what Jesus restored we need to understand what was there in the first place. God created the garden and placed Adam in it and met Him there (Genesis 2).

Adam walked and talked with God and God walked and talked with him. The original sin caused a separation in that fellowship and the Holy Spirit was taken from man (Genesis 3).

God established a system in the Old Testament where He dwelled in the Tabernacle, in the Holy of Holies. His Holy Spirit was now confined to the Ark of the Covenant and the only person that had access to this presence was the High Priest, and only once a year, on the Day of Atonement. By the time that Jesus came on the scene, the temple had been rebuilt.

The Ark of the Covenant was now in an elaborate temple and the Holy of Holies was behind a massive curtain.

Once again, only one person had the authority to go pass this curtain and into the presence of God. Our text teaches us that when Jesus cried His last cry and gave up His spirit, the curtain was split from top to bottom. For the first time in the history of the Jewish covenant, the Holy Spirit was loosed from the confines of the tabernacle.

Fifty days later, on the Day of Pentecost, that same Holy Spirit was poured out (Acts 2) upon believers and the New Testament church was birthed.

Summary

When you are a born-again believer, you are now that same temple referred to in 1 Corinthians 3:16 and the Holy Spirit now lives inside of you. Your body is the outer court, your soul is the inner court, and your Spirit is the Holy of Holies. God Himself, lives inside of you and that access was given to us through Jesus' work on the cross.

Jesus also said in John 14:13, 14 that we could now come to the Father in His name and receive. Jesus gave us the access to the Father in His name in prayer and the access to the Holy Spirit with His death.

Are you maximizing your benefits in Christ? Are you using your access? If not, it is time to make some changes! Spend time in prayer to the Father and fellowship with the Spirit.

CONFESSION

Heavenly Father, I can boldly confess the Word of God in the name of Jesus and know that You hear me. I have repented of my sin and accepted Jesus as my Lord. I am covered by His blood and anointed by His Spirit. The Holy Spirit lives in me and I am the new temple and walk in this new Kingdom. I utilize my access to You Father and stake a claim on my benefits. I am healed, healthy, blessed, and prosperous in everything I put my hands to do! In Jesus' name, Amen!

4. PEACE OF GOD

Philippians 4:6, 7 "Be careful for nothing; but in everything by prayer and supplication with thanksgiving let your requests be made known unto God. 7And the peace of God, which passeth all understanding, shall keep your hearts and minds through Christ Jesus."

Philippians 4:6, 7 (AMPV) - "Do not fret or have any anxiety about anything, but in every circumstance and in everything, by prayer and petition (definite requests), with thanksgiving, continue to make your wants known to God."

Paul teaches us that that same access to God in prayer unleashes a supernatural peace in our lives. The text very clearly tells us not to worry about anything, but to pray about everything. When we worry, it is an indication that we do not trust God. If we truly trust God, then we will not worry. Worry and prayer are counterproductive. *"God would keep us in 'perfect peace"* (Isaiah 23:6)

When we keep our minds on Him (prayer), because we are indicating that we trust Him. Paul simply tells us to pray, not to worry, and to receive a peace that no one can completely understand. God's peace is truly beyond explanation.

It is something that you have either experienced and can identify with or have not experienced and are clueless about. This peace is so awesome, the text says, that it actually controls the way we think and feel.

Summary

1. Worry is the fruit, but unbelief is the root: When you worry, it is because you do not believe God.

2. Combat worry with prayer and trust: When you pray to the Father, in the name of Jesus, and in accordance with the Word, you must have the faith that God will bring it to pass. This faith will eradicate the worry and release God's supernatural peace.

3. Receive God's peace and allow it to control the way you think and feel: After prayer, receive God's peace and walk in it.

Thoughts of doubt and unbelief will invariably come, but we do not have to receive them. Cast the impure thoughts away and allow the peace of God to control the way you think and feel.

4. Stake a claim on your benefits: In the natural, if you were educated on a new benefit of citizenship in your earthly country, you would still have to go down to the respective office and stake a claim on that benefit.

In the Spirit, it works the same way. I have educated you on this benefit, but you still have to go to the Father in prayer and stake a claim on your benefit.

5. Education does not guarantee application: Many people know about benefits they can claim, but they are too lazy to go and make a demand on those same benefits. Peace is one of the benefits of becoming a child of God and operating in His Kingdom. Will you stake your claim today?

CONFESSION

Heavenly Father, I am born-again. I am a citizen of Your Kingdom. I stake a claim on my benefits. I know through the Word of God that peace is a benefit. I claim MY peace today. I walk in Your peace, the peace that passes all understanding. I allow your peace to control the way I think and feel. When I come in contact with other people today no matter how I am treated, I will not lose my peace. I will not allow worry and unbelief to seep into my life. In Jesus' name Amen!

5. PRESENCE OF GOD

Joshua 1:5 "There shall not any man be able to stand before thee all the days of thy life: as I was with Moses, so I will be with thee: I will not fail thee, nor forsake thee."

Presence! Oh, the magnitude and power in the presence of God! There is so much to this benefit that I felt compelled to share it with you in this booklet even though I cannot possibly convey it all. Joshua is an excellent example of having and experiencing the presence of God. It was a direct promise from God Himself!

Joshua was called by God to take over as leader after Moses died and he was to lead the nation of Israel into the Promised Land. He and Caleb were the only two of his generation that would cross over into the Promised Land for this reason: they were the only two of the entire nation of Israel that had the faith that they could go over and possess the land promised to them and conquer the giants that were living there. 10 of the 12 spies sent into the land came back and spoke in fear when they reported to the nation of Israel about the inhabitants (giants) that possessed their promise, but Joshua and Caleb spoke in faith.

They were able to speak in faith because of the presence of the Lord in their lives and that same presence would now enable Joshua to lead the nation of Israel (finally) into the Promised Land.

Summary:

1. Fear vs. Faith: I have said many times that fear moves satan and faith moves God. God honors faith and wants us to look at insurmountable circumstances and speak victory, in His name, by faith. God oftentimes places us in situations that are bigger than our ability. These situations require faith. The choice is ours, however, to operate therein. If we choose to operate in fear and say that it is too hard and the giants are too big, then we will never receive the promises of God.

If we operate in faith and say that in spite of the obstacle and in spite of the size of the giants, we will be able to overtake the land in the name of Jesus; then we will have what we say! What giants stand in your way this morning? What situation will require you to operate in faith today? Remember that you will have to choose to either operate in fear and fail or operate in faith and succeed.

2. Love casts our fear: We can now see that fear is the enemy of faith. We must combat fear in every area of our lives. When we worry, we are telling God that we don't trust Him.

Our God wants to know that we trust Him in where we are now before He takes us to where we need to be.

John said, "There is no fear in love; but perfect love casteth out fear: because fear hath torment. He that feareth is not made perfect in love." (1 John 4:18) So we cannot walk in perfect love and fear at the same time. Perfect love eradicates fear.

3. God is Love: This is the key. John also said in John 4:8, "He that loveth not knoweth not God; for God is love." So we now see that:

(A) Fear is the enemy of faith,
(B) Love casts our fear,
(C) God is love.

So when we look at our text again we will see that God promised Joshua (and us) that He would never give up on him and never leave him.

In this light we can deduce that we are:

(A) Promised the presence of God
(B) His presence brings with it His love
(C) His love casts out every fear
(D) When we do not operate in fear, we can freely operate in faith and overcome every obstacle and conquer every giant!

Are you ready to face giants today with the presence of the Lord?

CONFESSION

Heavenly Father, You are here with me today and will always be with me! Your presence brings with it Your Power, Your Protection, Your Peace, and Your Love! Perfect love casts our fear. I do not operate in fear, but in faith. In faith, and with your presence, I am able to overcome every hindrance and conquer every giant! Your presence guarantees me the victory! In Jesus' name Amen!

6. AUTHORITY

Luke 9:1 "Then he called his twelve disciples together, and gave them power and authority over all devils, and to cure diseases."

There is a movie entitles "Walking Tall". In the movie, Dwayne Johnson (The Rock) plays an ex-soldier turned sheriff, who is trying to clean up his town. The first thing that he does after becoming sheriff is to fire all of his corrupt deputies.

He is then left without any deputies to help carry out his vision and his duties for the town. He drives to meet one of his childhood friends, played by Johnnie Knoxville, and deputizes him by giving him a badge. This badge now authorizes Johnnie to operate on behalf of the sheriff. The badge also gives him the right to govern over the law-breakers in the town. In similar fashion, Jesus called His disciples together to help Him carry out His vision and duties for the world. They had watched Him as He healed the sick and ministered to the needy, but He would now transfer authority to His followers.

This authority gave them the right to operate on His behalf and legal ability to exercise judgment over devils and diseases.

Devils signify spiritual oppression and diseases signify physical infirmity. Jesus released the authority over both!

Summary

1. The same power and authority released to the disciples has been released to us: Jesus suffered, bled, died, and was buried; but God raised Him from the dead with all power in His hand. This power and authority is now transferred to all believers at the point of salvation.

When we are born-again, the Holy Spirit comes into our lives (Ephesians 1:13) and the blood of Jesus is applied to our sin (Hebrews 9:22). The Holy Spirit and the blood release the power and the authority.

2. We have been deputized: (Luke 10:19) The Holy Spirit is our weapon (which we will discuss later) and the blood of Jesus is our badge. Just like the badge deputized the sheriff's friend in the movie, the blood deputizes us in real life. We now have the legal right and authority to operate in the Kingdom and on behalf of Jesus. This authority is released from heaven, but intended to be exercised in the earth.

3. We can rule over both the external and the internal: The text teaches us that this authority releases us to rule over:

(A) The devil and demons, which represent external attacks and spiritual oppression

(B) Diseases, which represent internal infirmities and physical sickness. God wants us to rightly rule over every attack, external or internal, and to freely flow in His authority; that the world may know that after 2,000 years, Christ is still the answer!

Do you know better understand your benefits? You have been deputized by Jesus to operate on His behalf in the earth. Are you ready to carry out your duties today? You have the legal right to rule over devils and diseases.

Now get up and allow God to use you this day for His service **that divine resources may meet human needs!**

CONFESSION

Heavenly Father, I am a born-again believer. The Holy Spirit is my weapon and the Blood of Jesus is my badge. You have given me the power and authority to tread on serpents and scorpions, and over all the power of the enemy. Nothing shall by any means hurt me, because I walk in your authority. In Jesus' name Amen!

7. HEALTHING

Exodus 15:26; "And said, If thou wilt diligently hearken to the voice of the LORD thy God, and wilt do that which is right in his sight, and wilt give ear to his commandments, and keep all his statutes, I will put none of these diseases upon thee, which I have brought upon the Egyptians: for I *am* the LORD that healeth thee."

Psalms 107:20; "He sent his word, and healed them, and delivered *them* from their destructions."

Isaiah 53:5; "But he *was* wounded for our transgressions, *he was* bruised for our iniquities: the chastisement of our peace *was* upon him; and with his stripes we are healed."

1 Peter 2:24; "Who his own self bare our sins in his own body on the tree that we, being dead to sins, should live unto righteousness: by whose stripes ye were healed."

The Scriptures teaches us that God is a healer, and healing is provided for us through the death, burial, and resurrection of our Lord and Saviour Jesus Christ. When a Christians experiencing symptoms of sickness, we must recognize that it is not of God, but the devil trying to get us to receive something that is not of God.

When Christians experience the symptoms of sickness, we are to lay claim own the benefit of healing that is provided through the covenant. When we pray the prayer of faith for healing God unleashes a supernatural healing in our lives. The text very clearly tells us that healing belongs to us. When we prayer, we are claim our benefit of healing we are showing God that we are trust Him.

Summary

1. One of the names of God is JEHOVAH - RAPHA "The Lord our healer"

2. Sickness and diseases - Come from the devil who is an enemy of God who comes to steal, kill, and destroy God's creation, and people of God are his number one target.

3. Combat sickness and diseases with prayer and trust: When you pray to the Father, in the name of Jesus, and in accordance with the Word, you must have the faith that God will bring it to pass. This faith will eradicate sickness and diseases, and release God's supernatural of healing.

4. Stake a claim on your benefits: In the natural, if you were educated on a new benefit of citizenship in your earthly country, you would still have to go down to the respective office and stake a claim on that benefit.

In the Spirit, it works the same way. I have educated you on this benefit, but you still have to go to the Father in prayer and stake a claim on your benefit.

CONFESSION

Heavenly Father, I am born-again. I am a citizen of Your Kingdom. I stake a claim on my benefits. I know through the Word of God that healing is a benefit. I claim MY healing today. I walk in my healing, the healing that only you has provided. I allow your Word to control the way I think and feel. When I come in contact with other people today no matter how I am treated, I will not lose my healing. I will not allow doubt and unbelief to seep into my life. By the stripe of Jesus I am healed. In Jesus' name Amen!

8. THE POWER

Acts 1:8 "But ye shall receive power, after that the Holy Ghost is come upon you: and ye shall be witnesses unto me both in Jerusalem, and in all Judaea, and in Samaria, and unto the uttermost part of the earth."

The word translated "power" is the Greek word *dunamis*. This is the root word for our English word dynamite. Like dynamite, it is loaded and explosive, but only when ignited. Dynamite can be stored safely for years without it ever doing anything. If the dynamite is ever ignited, however, then it immediately affects itself and its environment. The atmosphere around the dynamite feels the effects of the blast and is impacted by its power.

Summary:

1. God has given us both the right (authority) and the power.

2. We receive this power (dynamite power) when we receive God's Holy Spirit.

3. The power of the Holy Spirit has the propensity to affect us and everything around us, but if not ignited, it can remain dormant for years.

4. One of the benefits that we have as born-again believers is this power that can change us and help change those around us. This power gives us the ability to effectively witness (share the gospel) in the midst of difficult circumstances.

5. God would never equip us with this power if He did Not intend for us to use it. We must use it to help bring about change in our lives and then allow that change to be exhibited to others so that they can experience the same.

6. Information is the first step, but if not coupled with application, it will never bring about change in your life. Now that you know you have access to life changing power, in the Holy Spirit, what are you going to do about it? Will you go on with life as usual, or will you ask the Father, in the name of Jesus, to unleash this power to bring about change in your life and the lives of others?

7. Paul taught us in Ephesians 3:20 "Now unto him that is able to do exceeding abundantly above all that we ask or think, according to the power that worketh in us,"

The key here is that the Holy Spirit is WITHIN us. We don't need to wait on anything else. We received everything we would ever need when we received the Holy Spirit.

If you always do what you always did, you will always get what you always got. Are you ready for a change?

CONFESSION

Heavenly Father, I am a born-again believer. I understand my benefits and I stake claim to those benefits today. You have given me the power, in the Holy Spirit, to bring about change in my life. I tap into that power and pronounce that I am delivered from every yoke of bondage and walk in freedom and liberty. I also share this liberty with others, that they may receive it as well. I will never be the same. In Jesus' name Amen!

9. THE ANOINTING.

Isaiah 10:27 "And it shall come to pass in that day, hat this burden shall be taken away from off thy shoulder, and his yoke from off thy neck, and the yoke shall be destroyed because of the anointing."

The Anointing! Isaiah prophesied that the Israelites would encounter a day where the burdens would be removed from their shoulders and the yokes from upon their necks and the yokes then being literally destroyed. This burden-removing and yoke-destroying power would come by something called "the anointing."

In the Old Testament, the Levitical priesthood would anoint people or things with oil. This oil was representative of the Holy Spirit. There were some who were actually "anointed" by the Holy Spirit. Those in the Old Testament received their anointing for a specific task. Commonly, the Holy Spirit would come upon the chosen individual and use him/her for the time. This was not necessarily a permanent condition. We now fast-forward to the New Testament.

We know that Jesus was baptized by John in the Jordan. When He came up out of the water, the Holy Spirit came down in the form of a dove and "anointed" Him.

Jesus lived in seeming obscurity for the 30 years prior to His baptism. Something happened, however, after He was anointed by the Holy Spirit.

The Bible then begins to add an addendum to His name and it begins to refer to Him as the Christ. Christ is not Jesus' last name. Christ literally means "Anointed One." Fast-forward now to today. Born-again believers today are called Christians, which literally means "Anointed like Christ" or "Anointed Ones."

Summary

It is important for us to understand the power of the "anointing," as we come together corporately to believe God for burdens being removed and yokes being destroyed over the lives of those in our community and nation.

Golden nuggets:

1. The Old Testament anointing oil was symbolic and the Holy Spirit came upon men temporarily.

2. In the New Testament, the Holy Spirit is the anointing Himself and He comes into the lives of believers permanently.

3. It is not the will of God that we walk around burdened down with worry and yoked with sin. One of the key benefits of life in Christ is to be delivered from burdens and yokes. God wants us to be free and enjoy our freedom in Him!

Are you ready to be free? Stake a claim on this benefit - the anointing. Believe God for deliverance from every addiction and freedom from every yoke.

CONFESSION

Heavenly Father, I am a born-again believer. I am anointed like Christ. I cast my cares upon You, God, because you care for me. You remove my burdens and destroy every yoke in my life. I receive freedom and I walk in it daily. I am free! In Jesus' name Amen!

10. DIVINE PROTECTION

Isaiah 54:17 "No weapon that is formed against thee shall prosper; and every tongue that shall rise against thee in judgment thou shalt condemn. This is the heritage of the servants of the LORD, and their righteousness is of me, saith the LORD."

Protections! Our calendar used to be measured by life prior to Christ (B.C.) and life after Christ (A.D.). September 11th, 2001 changed that. Many now categorize our present age as life "Pre-" or "Post- September 11th". We know what happened on that day and how thousands of lives were snuffed out and the waves of fear that the events generated all over the world.

People were (and many still are) afraid to get on planes, open mail, and work in large buildings. Since then, we have deployed troops to Afghanistan, Qatar, Kuwait, Iraq, and Haiti (just to same a few). We should pray and confess God's protection over our military members and all leaders (government and military) at all levels, consistently.

This protection is not a hope, wish or desire; but rather a right and benefit of our new citizenship in the Kingdom of God.

Protection is available, but we must stake a claim on this benefit.

Summary:

1. Protection from weapons: Isaiah knew that Israel and the church would encounter many attacks from the enemy as indicated in our text verse above. The previous verse (v.16) deals with the blacksmith going to great lengths to form skilled weapons to rise up against them. These swords, javelins, daggers, etc.; may be formed, but they would not prosper against the children of God.

Application: Today we know that we do not wrestle against flesh and blood (Ephesians 6:10-18), but are in a spiritual battle. Just as the blacksmith spent countless hours in front of the fire forming weapons to destroy the nation of Israel, the enemy today spends countless hours devising plans of attack against us. He forms many weapons and formulates many plans, but we can find peace in knowing that we have the protection of God. Not ONE of these weapons will prosper against us. God will not stop them from being formed, but He will stop them from prospering against us.

2. Protection from slander: We know that there is power of death and life in the tongue (Proverbs 18:21). Just like the enemy forms physical and spiritual weapons against us, he also seeks to attack us through false accusations.

False accusations can cripple a leader, just as quickly as a bullet.

Petition: Our text teaches us that God will condemn every tongue that rises up against us in judgment. Not only will God protect us from the spiritual and physical attacks of the enemy, but we also have a right to protection from verbal attacks.

3. Receiving our Inheritance: A good man leaves an inheritance for his children (Proverbs 13:22). Man cannot be greater than God. God also leaves an inheritance of righteousness for His children. Our text teaches us that this protection is part of our heritage.

Petition: We don't have to wait on anything external to happen for us to claim this inheritance. Normally, you have to wait for your parent to die. Well, Jesus already died and was raised up from the dead. We can stake a claim on our inheritance right now!

One of our blessed benefits of life in Christ is protection. Are you ready to claim it today?

CONFESSION

Heavenly Father, You are a Righteous God and you leave an inheritance for your children. I am your child and have been born into Your family. I have a right to that inheritance and stake claim on your protection today. No weapon that is formed against me will prosper and every tongue that rises up against me, you will condemn! In Jesus' name Amen!

11. REVELATION

Jeremiah 33:3 "Call unto me, and I will answer thee, and show thee great and mighty things, which thou knowest not"

Revelation Knowledge! Jeremiah was a prophet and needed to hear from God clearly to be His mouthpiece in the earth for the Jewish people. You may not be a prophet, but you do have access to the Father, in the name of Jesus, and can receive divine revelation from God. The words translated 'marvelous and wondrous' in our text literally mean inaccessible and hidden things.

It is God's will that His children prosper (3 John 1:2) and live as examples of righteousness in the earth. Our success must be rooted and guided by the Word of God, not only the written word, but also the living revelation from the Father. God can show us things about ourselves, our surroundings, our future, etc.; that we could not learn any other way.

Remember that our future is God's past. Just like a builder has to finish the plans for a building before he ever gets started on the work, God's plan for our lives was finished before we ever came on the scene. So everything in our future is already in His past.

He knows the thoughts we have before we think them (Psalm 139), He knows the concerns we have before we feel them, and He knows the snares we will face before we encounter them.

Summary:

1. God knows everything: Before we will ever ask God to reveal anything to us, we must settle in our minds that He has what it is that we are asking for. You will never ask a homeless person for a million dollars.

Why? Because you will perceive that they do not have the ability to fulfill the request. For us to even pray to God, we must first believe in our hearts that he can make our prayer a reality. So, we must settle in our minds that God knows everything -- **period** -- before we begin to ask Him for information and revelation.

2. God is willing to share His wisdom with His children: Do you have children? If you do, then it is easy for you to relate to this concept. You want the best for your children and you are more than willing to sit down with them and teach them the way that they should go.

You don't want them to fail, so you attempt to equip them with the best possible information. You are willing to freely give everything you have learned through the years to your children. Now, if mere human beings are willing to do that for their natural children, how much more will God reveal to His children?

3. We must ask and ask in faith: God is willing to fulfill our request for information and other things as well, but when we come to Him, we must come in faith. He honors faith and is moved by it. Fear moves satan, but faith moves God.

James said it this way, "If any of you lack wisdom, let him ask of God, that giveth to all men liberally, and upbraideth not; and it shall be given him. But let him ask in faith, nothing wavering. For he that wavereth is like a wave of the sea driven with the wind and tossed." (James 1:5, 6)

Think about it. God, the Master and Creator of all things, and He is willing to share His wisdom with you. This is a tremendous benefit of being a citizen of the Kingdom.

Are you ready to stake a claim on this benefit?

CONFESSION

Heavenly Father, You know everything. I come in faith and stake a claim on the benefit of revelation. You can reveal to me hidden wisdom and actionable information. I ask and receive your wisdom, revelation, and knowledge today; concerning my family, career, destiny, and even my enemies. Show me, Lord, Your will and I will walk in obedience with what I receive. In Jesus' name Amen!

Section II

The Nature of a Covenant

The Nature of a Covenant

In order to understand and fully appreciate our Kingdom benefits as children of The Most High God, we must first understand the concept of *"covenant"*. It is because of God's covenant with us as His children, that we even have Kingdom citizenship benefits to claim. So, before we establish what several of those benefits are, let us ensure that we understand the "how" and "why" of the concept upon which our Kingdom citizenship is based.

A covenant is a special type of relationship in which two people enter into an alliance involving a firm commitment to one another and which usually makes demands on each party.

The Bible uses just two words for "covenant" that occur 313 times in 295 verses.

In fact, the Old and New "Testaments" are really the Old and New "Covenants" - the new covenant being that which was established by Christ through His shed blood for the remission of sins (Matthew 26:28). Marriage is referred to as "the covenant of God" in Proverbs 2:17.

This is the pattern followed in the Biblical picture of God's relationship with Israel. It is always made clear that the initiative is God's - that He makes covenants with His people and not vice versa, and that He is the superior party in the covenant. In the Old Testament, God promises His protection and His commitment to Israel, in return for which Israel must pledge to worship and serve Him alone, living in conformity with His moral and social standards.

This does not mean that God's covenant is necessarily conditional. There are certainly obligations laid upon Israel. Israel must worship the Lord alone and be loyal to Him in every sphere of life. Israel must be God's witness to all the nations. However, at heart, the covenants are not *based* on Israel's response to God, although this is not only expected but demanded.

The covenants of God are based completely on God's gracious and sovereign choice of Israel.

They are always based on God's prior grace and will, and they always make demands on the people involved in terms of how they must live their lives now that they are in a relationship with the God of Abraham, Isaac and Jacob.

This does not apply just to Israel, but to the Church also. The New Testament contains many obligations on Christians, and many passages like the following,

- "If you love me, you will obey what I command." (John 14:15).
- "You are my friends if you do what I command." (John 15:14).
- "Faith without deeds is dead." (James 2:26).

This is how we know that we love the children of God: by loving God and carrying out his commands (I John 5:2).

This new covenant is, of course, that which Jesus has brought about. Hebrews 8 explains that Jesus is the High Priest and mediator of this new covenant. It is also founded on better promises.

Hebrews 9 explains that Christ has obtained eternal redemption, and has enabled us to serve the living God. He was sacrificed to take away the sins of the people, and He will return a second time, not to bear sin, but to bring salvation for those who are waiting for Him.

In the New Testament, God's methodology is different. The nations are to be drawn toward God as the Church goes to the nations to proclaim His works. After Abraham died, Isaac inherited the promises. Isaac did not see the complete fulfillment of the promise, nor did Jacob who inherited them next (Hebrews 11:9).

The promises were inherited by Israel (*Romans 9:4-5*) and although flourishing under certain kings, Israel did not see the complete fulfillment of God's promises to Abraham. So what happened to them? It was the Lord Jesus who finally inherited the promises made to Abraham centuries before. However, the One who finally inherited the promises died, and so once more, the promises were available. When someone had died, it was necessary for their testament to be administered:

"For where there is a testament, there must also of necessity be the death of the testator. For a testament is in force after men are dead, since it has no power at all while the testator lives." (Hebrews 9:16-17).

So, Jesus rose from the dead and became the legal administrator of His own testament. "And for this reason He is the Mediator of the New Covenant by means of death, for the redemption of the transgressions under the first covenant, that those who are called may receive the promise of the eternal inheritance." (Hebrews 9:15).

When Jesus died, those who were of the faith of Abraham inherited the promises:

"So then those who are of faith are blessed with believing Abraham." (Genesis 3:9).

"And if you are Christ's, then you are Abraham's seed, and heirs according to the promise." (Galatians 3:29).

The apostle Paul understands of God's covenant with Abraham was the background of the great revelation that the Lord had given to Him, which he summarized in *Romans 4:13-16* which states:

"For the promise that he [Abraham] would be the heir of the world was not to Abraham or to his seed through the law, but through the righteousness of faith…"

Abraham received the promise that he would inherit the world. However, it was the seed of Abraham - Jesus Christ - who really inherited the world. This fact was foretold prophetically in Psalm 2:7-8(NKJV).

"I will declare the decree; the Lord has said to me, you are my son, today I have begotten you. Ask of me and I will give the nations for your inheritance and the ends of the earth for your possessions."

When Jesus rose from the dead and was seated at the right hand of the Father, He received His inheritance:

"Then Jesus came and spoke to them, saying, "All authority has been given to me in heaven and on earth". (Matthew 28:18).

However, in Christ, believers have become joint heirs and have therefore also inherited the world. This is a staggering thought! Even though the whole world lies under the sway of the wicked one (I John 5:19), according to God the legal owner of the world is Christ and His Church.

When Jesus gave the Great Commission to go into all the world, He was commanding the Church to go into all the nations and to inherit them as a fulfillment of God's promise made to Abraham. The Great Commission was not an afterthought but it is the divine way of fulfilling this momentous covenant.

It is my hope and prayer that you now understand the concept of "covenant" upon which your Kingdom citizenship benefits are based. Armed with this new knowledge, be encouraged to not only know your benefits, rights, and privileges as a child of God, but claim them and walk in them on a daily basis. Psalm 103:1-5, says "…forget not all his benefits:"

A Continuation of Claiming your Covenant Citizenship Benefits And Inheritance

12. MERCY

Lamentations 3:22, 23 "It is of the LORD's mercies that we are not consumed, because his compassions fail not They are new every morning: great is thy faithfulness."

Mercy! There are many songs that we sing in church. One of my favorite songs tells of God's grace and mercy. Grace is unmerited favor and mercy is loving kindness. Basically, grace is God giving us what we do not deserve and mercy is God not giving us what we do deserve.

If we would be honest with ourselves, we would have to admit that we have done enough wrong in our lives to deserve to go straight to hell. Our text tells us that it is simply through God's love (mercy) that we have not come to destruction. His mercies have no limit. The text then teaches us that God is faithful to provide us with brand new mercy every morning.

Summary:

1. **We are saved by grace**: I believe in holiness and believe that we should make every attempt to abstain from sin, but don't ever make the mistake of thinking that you are 'good enough' to make it to heaven. We all come short of the glory of God (Romans 3:23,24), but God has justified us (made us right) and redeemed us (paid the price) by His grace. We are saved by grace and not by works, so that no one would have a right to boast (Ephesians 2:8,9).

Petition: Thank God every day for His wonderful kindness showered upon us. He gave us a gift that we did not deserve and paid a price that He did not owe.

2. We are kept by mercy: Born-again believers are not sinless (1 John 1:8), but we should not practice sin. Sin should not be our way of life. Whenever we do sin, however, it is because of God's tender mercies that we are not destroyed.

Petition: Thank God every day for His mercy. If it had not been for mercy, I would not be writing this booklet and you would not be reading it. We are here, because God loved us enough to look beyond our faults and see our need.

3. We are blessed to live our destiny out in increments: The text says that His mercies are new every morning. God has destined us and has plans to give us an expected end (Jeremiah 29:11), but He blessed us to live out our lives in increments of days.

David said in Psalm 119:24 "This is the day that the Lord has made…" He did not say that this was the week, nor month, nor year. Our lives are segmented into days and His mercies are renewed every day!

Petition: When I was a kid, we used to play marbles and when you made a mistake you would say "Slippers!" and this would mean you got to do it over – a "do over". In real life, we cannot live yesterday over and literally get a 'Do Over' for a bad day, but we can 'Start Over' the next morning!

Could you imagine how terrible it would be to live life as ONE LONG DAY! Praise God that He has blessed us to live our lives in increments of days. We know where we are and we know where we want to head (our destiny), and God has blessed us to attempt to get there day by day!

What a wonderful benefit of our new citizenship -- mercy! **Yesterday ended last night!** Move forward and not backward. We serve of a God of progression and not regression. **The best is yet to come!**

CONFESSION

Heavenly Father, I thank you for your grace and praise You for Your mercy. This is a brand new day and I walk in brand new mercy. I do not have to face this day's issues with yesterday's mercy. Yesterday ended last night. I look forward and not backward. This is the day that you have made and I will rejoice and be glad in it! In Jesus' name Amen!

13. FAITH

2 Corinthians 5:7 "For we walk by faith, not by sight"

Faith! Faith is something that most people would not look at as a benefit of the Kingdom, but it is a tremendous benefit. Let me explain. If you asked me to come by your house this Saturday morning and I said, "I will try to make it," then the best that you can do is HOPE that I will show up.

Hope is open-ended because it is not tied to a promise. On the other hand, if I said, "I promise I will be there," then you can have faith that I will show up. Even after I promised that I would show up, however, I still might not make it because I am a man and prone to mistakes.

God, however, is not a man (Numbers 23:19) and if He promised something, He will do it -- period! The benefit of faith, then, is tied to the Word of God. The reason I share God's Word is because I want people to be able to add substance to their hope (Hebrews 11:1) and walk in faith. We don't have to live by open-ended wishes, but our text tells us that we should walk by faith!

Summary:

How can we apply this faith to our daily lives? Let's break it down:

1. Find the right promise: Jesus spoke to people who were hungry and said, "I am the Bread" (John 6:35). Jesus spoke to a woman whose brother had just died and said, "I am the Resurrection and the Life" (John 11:25). Both were the truth. Both were the Word of God. Both were packed with promise and potential. But Jesus would not have told the people who were hungry that He was the Resurrection and He would not have told the woman dealing with death that He was the Bread.

Why? Because those words, although the truth, did not apply to the situation! The Bible is full of promises. I already taught you that you cannot have faith without a promise. Whatever situation you find yourself in, you must find a promise in the Word of God that applies to it!

2. Confess that promise: We have the power of death and life in our tongue (Proverbs 18:21). When we repeat God's Word over our situation, we loose authority in the earth for angels to operate on our behalf.

We give God earthly license for heavenly interference. Keep repeating that promise and believing that God will bring it to pass.

3. Develop a plan: Many people perform steps 1 and 2. They find the scripture and they confess it with their mouths, but then they wait and never do anything about it. We must ask the Holy Spirit to give us clear instructions on what our responsibilities are to bring to pass this promise in our lives. God will show us what our part is and He oftentimes waits for us to fulfill our part, BEFORE He does His.

4. **DO IT!** James said, "Faith without works is dead" (James 2:20). If you ask me, "How do we walk by faith?"

I will tell you:

(1) Find the promise in the Word of God,
(2) Confess that promise over your life,
(3) Develop a plan under the leadership of the Holy Spirit, and
(4) DO IT! You will never receive from God without actually DOING what He tells you to DO. We can talk about it all day long, but faith requires action!

The best the world can do is hope, but we can walk in faith because we have the Word of God. What a wonderful benefit! Are you ready to use this benefit this week?

CONFESSION

Heavenly Father, Your Word is power-packed with promises. I find the promise that applies to my current situation. I speak that Word and believe it will come to pass in my life. I am led of Your Spirit to develop a plan to bring it to fruition and I have the courage and the ability to DO what you tell me to DO. I walk by faith and not by sight. In Jesus' name Amen!

14. LIBERTY

Galatians 3:13 "Christ hath redeemed us from the curse of the law, being made a curse for us: for it is written, Cursed is every one that hangeth on a tree:"

Liberty! The Old Testament Law was the schoolmaster that taught us the frailties of humanity. The only person that ever fulfilled the Law was Jesus Christ. It was so strict that no human could actually live a perfect life by its rules. Paul said, in the verses leading up to our text, "But that no man is justified by the law in the sight of God, it is evident: for, The just shall live by faith. And the law is not of faith: but, The man that doeth them shall live in them." Galatians 3:11, 12

The person who lives in right relationship with God does so by embracing what God arranges for him. Doing things for God is the opposite of entering into what God does for you. Habakkuk had it right:

"The person, who believes God, is set right by God -- and that's the real life.'

Rule-keeping does not naturally evolve into living by faith, but only perpetuates itself in more and more rule-keeping, a fact observed in Scripture: The one who does these things [rule-keeping] continues to live by them. The Good News is that our text teaches us that Christ rescued us from the Law's curse and condemnation. He became a curse in our place.

Jesus was once asked which of all the commandments of the Law was the greatest. Check out His response: "Jesus said unto him, Thou shalt love the Lord thy God with all thy heart, and with all thy soul, and with all thy mind. This is the first and great commandment. And the second is like unto it, Thou shalt love thy neighbour as thyself." Matthews 22:37-39

Summary:

1. The Law was too strict for any human being to ever fulfill and thereby condemned us all.

2. Jesus lived a perfect life and fulfilled the Law.

3. Jesus exchanged His right with those (us) that did not deserve it.

4. Jesus simplified things for us. We are now to love God with all our heart, soul, and mind; and love others as much as we love ourselves.

5. God's Grace (unmerited favor) keeps us when we mess up.

6. God did all of this, so that we could be free and redeemed from the curse of the law.

7. One of the greatest benefits of our new citizenship is liberty! We have been made free by the blood of Jesus. He has made us righteous, even though – in ourselves we could never be. We should not allow anyone to condemn us after Christ has redeemed us.

Receive your liberty and walk in it. Do not entangle yourself again with sin. If you fall into sin, follow 1 John 1:9 which tells us to repent, confess our sin to God and move forward!

Are you a born-again believer? If so, then you must know that you have been made righteous by Christ and accept that fact, once and for all. Move forward and not backward.

Strive for progression and not regression. Settle in your mind that you are free and seek to enjoy your liberty in Christ!

CONFESSION

Heavenly Father, I am a born-again believer. I have been made the righteousness of God by faith. I am not under the law, nor its curse. I have been redeemed from the inevitable fate of the law and have been granted forgiveness because of the price that Jesus paid on Calvary's Cross! I am free and I walk in my liberty today and every day. I will never the same, never be the same! In Jesus' name Amen!

15. JOY

Philippians 4:4 "Rejoice in the Lord always: and again I say, Rejoice"

Joy! This is an often overlooked benefit to our Kingdom. In our previous kingdom (the world), the best we could have was happiness; and that kingdom promoted happiness and the pursuit of it, as a way of life.

The problem is that happiness comes from the English word *happenstance*, which is the same word for *circumstance*. So happiness is a result of happenings. If something good happens we can be happy, if something bad happens we can be sad. That is truly no way to live. You are up today and down tomorrow, happy this week and sad next week.

We live in an ever changing and often frustrating environment, so if our state of well-being is contingent upon circumstances, you can easily see that our lives will be an emotional roller-coaster. The good news is that we don't have to abide by the system of the old kingdom. Once we are born-again into the Kingdom of God, then we can learn about and apply His benefits.

One of the benefits of our life in this new Kingdom is the fruit of the Spirit (Galatians 5:22).

One of the fruits of the Spirit is joy. Joy is not happiness. Joy is a calm delight and an exceeding gladness. It is both quiet confidence and celebratory praise. It can be a gentle whisper or a colossal roar. It is both peace and power wrapped into one

This joy is inherent to the Holy Spirit. The Holy Spirit dwells in the lives of born-again believers. Since the Holy Spirit is always there for us to access, then His joy is always there for us to tap into.

Summary:

1. The best that our old kingdom can offer is happiness.

2. Happiness is a result of happenings.

3. Our new Kingdom offers joy, from the Holy Spirit, as one of its benefits.

4. As a born-again believer, I have the right to claim this benefit and the access to the Holy Spirit required tapping into it.

5. This joy can give me calm delight and quiet confidence; and also exceeding gladness and celebratory praise.

6. The old kingdom only offers happiness for good things that happen. After the good event is over, then that happiness is over. They can never re-happy!

7. The Holy Spirit is in me and I can always tap into His benefits. No matter how I feel and no matter how bad things may look, I can always tap into this joy. I can always re-joice, but the world can never re-happy!

Are you struggling with some issues in your life? Are you having a rough week? Are you frustrated here and there? Then why not tap into this benefit? It is your right as a citizen of the Kingdom of God to stake claim on your benefits.

CONFESSION

Heavenly Father, I am a born-again believer. I have been born into Your Kingdom and have a right to all the benefits therein. One of the benefits of this new Kingdom is joy. I stake a claim on this benefit this morning and declare that I walk in the joy of the Lord. I will not allow happenings to derail me from enjoying my joy! The Holy Spirit is with me and His joy overtakes me today and every day. I will never be the same. In Jesus' name Amen!

16. MILITARY MIGHT

Psalms 91:9-11 "Because thou hast made the LORD, which is my refuge, even the most High, thy habitation; There shall no evil befall thee, neither shall any plague come nigh thy dwelling. For he shall give his angels charge over thee, to keep thee in all thy ways"

Military Might! We all know that the United States is in the middle of an ongoing global war on terrorism. America's military members are in harm's way daily in Iraq, Kuwait, Afghanistan, and other places. By the way, please don't stop praying for them. In spite of the recent losses of lives, it is globally accepted that the United States has the strongest, best equipped, and best trained military in the world. One of the benefits of becoming a U.S. citizen is receiving the protection of the military.

When the U.S. sends out ambassadors to foreign nations, we do so with a certain level of military protection. There are U.S. Marines assigned to protect the Embassy, the Ambassador's house, and possibly even the Ambassador's movements.

If someone from that foreign country attacks the Ambassador, they know that it will be an international incident. The military force already deployed will react and those Marines also have the full power of the entire U.S. military behind them and are ready to move upon orders.

We are born-again into Christ, but we have to live in the world. We live in the world, but we are not of this world (John 15:19). We are ambassadors in a foreign land. (2 Corinthians 5:20)

We go to church (home) for training and equipping, but we then leave and go back to live out our training in our foreign land. If we are attacked in this foreign land (the world), it becomes an international incident. But like U.S. ambassadors, we are not without protection.

Summary:

1. We must recognize that the LORD Most High is our fortress and we find protection in Him and Him alone.
2. He commands His angels to protect us wherever we go.
3. This right to protection is given to all ambassadors (citizens) of Christ.
4. This protection is not earned by virtue of our works, but rather necessary by virtue of our position.
5. The greatest army anywhere is armed and ready to protect us and to ward off any attacks from the enemy.
6. As a citizen of heaven and an Ambassador of Christ, operating in a foreign land, this protection is one of our benefits.

Are you ready to face this day? Are you prepared for everything you will have to endure? I pray that you are better equipped for this day and more at rest now, knowing that you have a heavenly host of angels - armed and battle-ready - to protect you wherever you go.

CONFESSION

Heavenly Father, I am a born-again believer. I have declared my citizenship in Your Kingdom. I have a right to your protection. You are my fortress and you alone keep me from all hurt, harm or danger. I am Your Ambassador and I live in a foreign land. I stake claim to my right for protection and protection over my household this day and every day. In Jesus' name Amen!

17. STABILITY

2 Corinthians 4:8 "We are troubled on every side, yet not distressed; we are perplexed, but not in despair; Persecuted, but not forsaken; cast down, but not destroyed;"

Stability! Another reason that many people migrate to and seek to become citizens of the United States is for government stability. I know many may think that our government can be unstable at times, but in comparison with many other countries, we are a rock. Governments all over the world (ex. Haiti, Somalia) experience rises and falls due to corrupt politics and military coups.

This causes the citizens of those nations to experience fluctuating economical, social, and political climates; which cause many of them to endure hard times. Yes, many come to the Untied States looking for some semblance of normalcy and stability.

The greatest countries of this world, however, pale in comparison with the Kingdom of God. God is the same yesterday, today and forever (Hebrews 13:8). God cannot be overthrown, although satan tried. God cannot be voted out; He is a King and not an elected official.

God cannot be outsmarted; He is the Master of the Universe. God cannot be outshined; He is the source of all light. God is God and beside Him there is no other.

Summary:

1. We live in the world.

2. Those of us who are born-again are citizens of heaven and we simply live out our lives in this foreign land.

3. This world experiences a multitude of changes, causing us to experience some of those repercussions.

4. When we operate under Kingdom principles, we will be able to endure the changes and come out untouched.

5. Our text teaches us that we might suffer, but we are never crushed.

6. Our text teaches us that even when we don't know what to do, we never give up.

7. Our text teaches us that in times of trouble, God is always the same and He is always with us.

8. Our text teaches us that we might get knocked down, but we get back up again.

9. Isaiah said it this way, "When thou passest through the waters, I will be with thee; and through the rivers, they shall not overflow thee: when thou walkest through the fire, thou shalt not be burned; neither shall the flame kindle upon thee." (Isaiah 43:2)

10. So we can see that a tremendous benefit to being a citizen of the Kingdom of God is having the ability to live a stable life in the midst of an unstable environment.

Do you need some stability in your life? Are things going haywire? Do things seem like they are out of control? Then why not stake a claim on your benefits?

CONFESSION

Heavenly Father, I am a born-again believer. I have declared my citizenship in Your Kingdom. I have a right to stability. You are a God that changes not. I hold to Your Unchanging Hand today and every day and I enjoy the stability that comes from being connected to You and being born into Your Kingdom. The world may change around me, the rains may fall, the winds may blow, the floods may flow, but it will not effect me; because I am rooted and grounded on the Rock! In Jesus' name Amen!

18. GLOBAL FAMILY

Matthew 12:50 "For whosoever shall do the will of my Father which is in heaven, the same is my brother, and sister, and mother."

Global Family! Jesus dealt with many issues in Matthew 12. He was confronted by the Pharisees about breaking the Sabbath, casting out demons, and committing blasphemy. While Jesus was speaking to the Pharisees, His mother and brothers showed up.

The scene is described in Matthew 12:46-50. Someone told him, "Your mother and brothers are standing outside, wanting to speak to you." Jesus replied, "Who is my mother, and who are my brothers?" He then pointed to His disciples (followers) and said, "Here are my mother and my brothers... " We pick up our text as He continues to say **"Anyone who obeys my Father in heaven is my brother or sister or mother."**

Jesus did not misunderstand the fact that He had a natural family, but He further understood the importance of a Godly family. In the natural, we have mother and father, brothers and sisters, but Jesus clearly illustrated a bond between members of His Body (the Body of Christ) that was even tighter than natural ties. I grew up without a natural brother.

One of the greatest revelations I received when I first became a Christian was the fact that I now had brothers and sisters all over the world. This bond is not limited to race, creed, nor gender. All born-again believers have the same Daddy and are related by the same blood (Jesus').

Summary

1. We can find peace in our Godly family: The Pharisees of this world will always attempt to frustrate the work of God, as seen in Matthew 12. We can find strength and peace, like Jesus did, in our Godly Global Family.

2. We can have family fellowship: Like me, you may not have grown up with a natural brother or maybe a sister, but in the family of God, you have brothers and sisters everywhere! Make a decision to spend time with them and get to know them.

We can enjoy family favor: Just like you would go to the airport to pick up your natural siblings, open up your house to them, feed them, and even clothe them; I have experienced the same from my spiritual siblings many times over.

We have brothers and sisters in the Body of Christ all over the world ready and willing to be a blessing to me and available for me to be a blessing to them.

Having a global family is a tremendous benefit of our new citizenship in heaven. Are you going to enjoy this benefit or ignore it? Once again, the choice is yours!

CONFESSION

Heavenly Father, I am born-again into your family. You are my Father and every one of your sons and daughters are my brothers and sisters. I enjoy their fellowship and they enjoy mine. I get to know them and allow them to get to know me. I walk in family favor all over the world and enjoy the peace that comes from knowing that I am not alone! In Jesus' name Amen!

Understanding and Claiming your Covenant Citizenship Inheritance

Possessing our Inheritance
Introduction

When God created Adam, he gave him authority over the earth. This action made him ruler over all the earth and god of the earth or this world. Adam through disobedience caused the fall of mankind by eating from the tree of knowledge of good and evil. By choosing to disobey Adam lost his position, territory on the earth, and his governmental responsibilities. He handed them over to lucifer, the prince or ruler of the kingdom of darkness, who deceived Eve through the serpent who now is called Satan. The result of the fall mankind caused a curse to come upon the earth. Every person that is born in the earth is shaped with iniquity and conceived in sin (Psalm 51:5). Man is a sinful creature; therefore, no man is born without sin. Yet, God proved to us and showed us just how much he loves us; in spite of our sins by giving his only son in order for us to have eternal life.

God wants us to have a personal relationship with Him. Although, sin separates us from the relationship that God desires of us, we still have a choice to develop a personal relationship with God. But in order to do so we must repent and ask God to forgive us of our sins and receive Jesus Christ as our personal Savior and Lord.

See prior to our being born-again we were a creation of God, and once we made a decision to received the Lord Jesus Christ as our own personal Lord and Saviour. Our position changed, prior to being born-again we used to a child of the devil because of what Adam and Eve did, and the way we changed family was through receiving God's Son and that gave us privilege of becoming a son or daughter. (See John 1:12).

As we mature we grow from a babe in Christ, the becoming a Son or daughter in Christ, as continue our growth we come into the position of knowing who we are and what we have as a result of growth in the things of God, but when we were initially born into the family of God, we became heir of God, and joint heir with Jesus and it is only through growth that we understand what it means to be a heir or joint-heir. (See Galatians 4:1-7). According Psalm 36:8; Ephesians 1:13-14; He has given to us the Holy Spirit of promise as a down payment. As we mature we will be a position that we can enjoy or take part in our inheritance. See the inheritance only come when some dies, Jesus has already die and rose again, and He is ready to share inheritance with us because we are joint-heir with Him.

Now just in case you have never prayed the pray of salvation, It is listed for you, if you are not born-again you can become born-again.

Pray this pray now: Salvation

Dear Heavenly Father,

I come to you now and humbly ask for forgiveness. Lord I confess that I'm a sinner and I've broken your Holy law. I realize that the penalty of sin is death. I believe that Jesus Christ suffered and died on the cross to take the punishment for all my sins. I believe that Jesus rose from the dead and I accept Him as my personal Saviour, from this moment forward I give you my heart and trust you to be the Lord of my life. Please forgive all my sins and send Your Spirit to help me to do your will. I thank you for your great love and your gift of eternal life; I pray this in Jesus Name.

In praying the pray of salvation you automatically become a citizen of your Kingdom. You have been translated from the kingdom of darkness into the Kingdom of God. As a genuine born-again Christian, a citizen of the Kingdom of God you wants above everything else, to do the will of God. Don't be ashamed to witness to others and tell them how to become a Christian. Join a Bible believing Church and be water baptized as an act of faith to let the world know you are identifying the death, burial, and resurrection of Christ's.

1) New born baby in Christ: Romans 8:15-16; States once we are born-again, there is an inheritance for us, but it will not be delivered to us beyond our level of growth. Now an heir is a potential owner, meaning that there is something that's going to be passed down to them. Paul in his writing to the Galatians stated that a child is no different than servant.

2) A child of God: Romans 8:17; States that as a new born baby in the natural form needs milk to grow; According 1 Peter 2:1; "As new born babies in Christ, we are to desire the sincere milk of the Word of God that ye may grow thereby:" Basically what the Word of God is saying, is that the primary way for spiritual growth to occur is through the knowledge of the Word of God, so that we may apply to our life and grow there by. When we talk about the Word of God, we must remember that Jesus said that man shall not live by bread alone, but by every Word that proceedeth out of the mouth of God (Matthew 4:4), and knowledge gives strength (Proverbs 24:4).

You are not your flesh; your flesh is your house. The Word of God is food for your spirit. It is fine to get the sincere milk of the Word of God, *but the quality of your intake will determine the strength of your output*.

In talking about babies, it is difficult for babies to receive certain things because they are babies. In the natural world a parent will not give a young child a gun. Why? Because the young child is not developed enough or responsible enough to handle that gun and what comes with it.

You will find that the level of the Knowledge of God's Word that person is getting or has will be reflected in their ability to dominate the trials and storms of life. In nursing a baby, you give them milk first because they are a baby, but as you desire for them to grow, you will eventually give them some mash potatoes, small pieces of meat. The same thing is true for spiritual babies, the level of God's will determine your levels of growth, and God does not want us to stay on milk, because he desire that we grow also and become strong adult Christians spiritually.

According to 1 Corinthians 3:1-3; *what type of man or women are you?* Remember in Mark 4:35-41, they ask this question what type of man is He meaning Jesus? "What manner of man is this, that even the wind and the sea obey him?" They knew that He was not a mere man. As Christians we are not to be mere or carnal but mighty and spiritual men of God. See that is why the devil has been getting away with so much because Christians are acting as mere men or as carnal Christians.

The reason for this is found in Hebrews 5:12, and if we do not understand Hebrews 5:12, Ephesians 1:17-22 is clearer in the message. Satan will continue to dominate our lives and the reason for this is because we are still in babyhood state. In the church there are a many Christian babies, yet they may be adults in the natural form. The enemy gets away with a lot of the things because a mere man cannot defeat him nor stop him. See what needs to happen is that Christians are to grow up from babyhood state into being a child of God, and then to adulthood Christians.

3) You are ROYLATY seated together with Christ Jesus in heavenly *places*: In looking at Ephesians 2:6; this verse reveals our position in Christ and we must understand our position and operate from this position of being seated in heaven as one who has authority over the devil and the ability to make decrees, declarations and having all of heaven backing us as Christians when we speak the Word of God. (Isaiah 55:8-11).

In Acts 20:4; "And now, brethren, I commend you to God, and to the word of his grace, which is able to build you up, and to give you an inheritance among all them which are sanctified."

Remember before you can receive your inheritance you must be at a certain level maturity. According to Galatians 4:1-4; When we are born-again we are born as babies into a royal family, as member of this royal family we need training.

We as Christians must get training. For example looking at the royal family of England Prince William, Prince Harry and other members of the Royal Family they had to receive training. They were groomed (or trained) from birth even though they could not fully understand what their tutors were saying. Their tutors were speaking to them even before they could understand they are royalty. It was imperative for them to be told who they were royalty. And no age was too young for them to learn. We as Christians and citizens of the kingdom of God are kings and priest. The Bible talks about us as royalty (1 Peter 2:9). Now in this case, we need to be taught.

What the Bible tells us is indeed a fact that we have been adopted, according to Romans 8:15; now adoption as we know it has something to do with someone outside of the family, who really doesn't belong to the family but is adopted into the family.

In the scriptures, adoption has to do with the action of parents who adopt their own children into a place where a ceremony is given in which the minor son or daughter is formally initiated into full family status being vested with rights and privileges of an adult. It has to do with a family of that child whereby a tutor would excise authority until that child was adopted, and once the child is adopted then the child takes on status as an adult.

As he or she grows and takes on adult responsibilities, the church will have us go through foundation classes. The foundation classes are to give them what they need in terms of a basic understanding of the Kingdom of God. So they can then go into the world and not be tossed to and fro by the circumstance they encounter in this world.

The foundation classes are where the scriptures that you must have command of are taught. The adoptions has nothing to do with somebody outside the family, but it has all to do with the inside the family. We are being raised up to take over and to assume the duties of be full grown member of the family. See we are the royalty and the tutor is the Holy Spirit. He is inspiring me as an author in writing this book, to help teach you who you are in Christ. You are royalty if you have been born-again and the Holy Spirit is now teaching you how everything should be.

In other words the Holy Spirit is teaching you how you are to sit, how you are to talk, how to conduct yourself, how to behave and how to think. You are being taught how to do everything because these things don't automatically develop. You must be developed. God has to do this with all of us but once he does, you have finished the course.

You now have the behavior of a king inside of you. A king decrees things and when you decree things you expect them to be carried out. Your speech is going to change; when we were in the world, when we were under the devil rulership we talk the world talks, if we felt like cursing somebody out we did it and thought nothing of it.

Now that we are Christian according to Ephesians 4:29; "Let no corrupt communication proceed out of your mouth, but that which is good to the use of edifying, that it may minister grace unto the hearers. As Christians we are royalty, and with our status we are to represent the Kingdom of God so therefore, we are speak words of exhortation, comfort, encouragement and yes we are to correct people, but there is royal out a *diplomatic* way of doing it so it will reflect who we are rather than pulling us out of our character as child of God.

When we operate from our status of royalty things start happening for you, with that status you can receive some big things, with understanding of this status we will be tread a certain way, because our status we stand for certain things because we are seated with Christ in Heavenly places.

I. What was Jesus' Inheritance?

According to the scriptures (See Revelation 5:11-12), when Jesus returned to Heaven he received: Power, Riches, Wisdom, Strength, Honour, Glory, and Blessings. As we understand that Jesus stripped himself of Deity and came to earth as a mere man to show us how a man that is filled with and lead by the Holy Spirit could walk the earth and defeat the devil.

II. Two Aspects of Our Inheritance.

There are two aspects of our inheritance that are very important for us as believers to understand. Our inheritance in God is very important to us as believers because it defines our position in God and who we are in God. (See Ephesians 1:18-20)

The first aspect of our inheritance is the eternal scope and the second is the here and now. God wants the eyes of our understanding to be opened to both of these aspects.

A). Our Eternal Inheritance.

I believe it is very important for us to catch a glimpse of what our eternal inheritance will consist of, because it will help us to endure all that comes our way in this life. When we see the greater glory that is awaiting us (See Titus 3:7, 2 Corinthians 4:17) that gives us the power to continue on our journey to claiming our inheritance.

B). Our Spiritual Inheritance Here & Now.

Being a join-heir with Christ, means that we actually are in position to take part of His blessings right now, Christ has given us the Holy Spirit as a promise of down payment. (See Ephesians 1:13-14, Psalms 36:8).

III. Keys to Possessing Your Inheritance.

1. You must believe that they Belongs To you: "Power, riches, wisdom, strength, honour, glory, and blessing."

As you can see from the above list, there are many things that have been given to you to ensure your success. Not only to succeed but to enjoy so that you become productive and successful in fulfilling God's purpose and destiny for your lives. You have to meditate on these things so that you get God's word firmly established in your heart, believing that they actually do belong to you. We have to be like Abraham and not waiver at the promises that God has for us. (See Romans 4:20-21)

When someone has passed the next thing that takes place after the homegoing services are the reading of the will. All family members and whoever else might be included in the will are invited to the attorney's office for the reading of a will. (See Hebrews 9:15-17)

A) Read the Will!

As a Christian, you are the seed of Abraham! What does that mean? It means everything God promised him belongs to you. It has been passed down to you through Jesus. Abraham's blessings are your inheritance! It has been willed to you by the Word of God. So let us read the will today. Let us look in the Bible and find out how God treated Abraham, because that is how God has promised to treat us.

The first promise God made to Abraham was: "I will make of thee a great nation, and I will bless thee, and make thy name great; and thou shalt be a blessing: And I will bless them that bless thee, and curse him that curseth thee: and in thee shall all families of the earth be blessed." (See Genesis 12:2-3)

To fully grasp what God was saying here, you must realize when He blesses someone, He is not just telling them to have a good day. He is conferring upon them the power to increase and prosper in every area of life. In fact, according to W.E. Vine and Webster's dictionary, the true definition of BLESS is "to cause to prosper, to make happy, to bestow favor upon, to consecrate to holy purposes, to make successful, to make prosperous in temporal concerns pertaining to this life, to guard and preserve."

It was actually THE BLESSING of God that made Abraham rich! It caused him to prosper wherever he went.

B) Making a personal claim of the Promises of God

Financial prosperity was not the only benefit God's blessing brought Abraham. It also gave him the ability to overcome. Because God has declared that those who cursed Abraham would themselves be cursed, Abraham could conquer any enemy that came against him or his family.

You can see this fact borne out in Genesis 14. It tells of the time when Lot and his family were taken captive by wicked kings who made war on Sodom and Gomorrah. When Abraham received the news about his nephew, he did not sit around wringing his hands wishing there was something he could do.

"He armed his trained servants born in his own house, three hundred and eighteen, and pursued…and smote them…. And he brought back all the goods, and also brought again his brother Lot, and his goods, and the women also, and the people" (verses 14-16).

Imagine that! Abraham and his servants single-handedly whipped four kings and their armies and then recovered everything and everyone they had taken captive! What gave Abraham the boldness to go after those kings? He knew he had a covenant with God. He knew God had promised to be an enemy to his enemies and he dared to act on that promise. Abraham understood that God was God! Abraham took God at His Word when He said, "Fear not, Abram: I am thy shield, and thy exceeding great reward" (See Genesis 15:1).

We need to do the same thing. We need to take that promise and put our name in it. After all it is ours! We are the seed of Abraham. As citizens of the Kingdom of God we qualify to receive an Inheritance Genesis 15:1 should be read like this: Fear not, (*Put in your name*). God is your shield, your abundant compensation, and your reward shall be exceedingly great!

God keeps His promises, and He promised Abraham that He would bless his seed. He said: "I will make thee exceeding fruitful, and I will make nations of thee, and kings shall come out of thee. And I will establish my covenant between me and thee and thy seed after thee in their generations for an everlasting covenant, to be a God unto thee, and to thy seed after thee" (See Genesis1 7:6-7)

C) You've Inherited It All!

God wanted you to be so sure that you have inherited it all that, He gave you a double guarantee. He not only gave His promise, He backed it with an oath: For when God made [His] promise to Abraham, He swore by Himself, since He had no one greater by whom to swear, saying, Blessing I certainly will bless you and multiplying I will multiply you. Accordingly God, in His desire to show more convincingly and beyond doubt to those who were to inherit the promise the unchangeableness of His purpose and plan intervened with an oath.

This was done by two unchangeable things [His promise and His oath], in which it is impossible for God ever to prove false or deceive us, we who have fled [to Him] for refuge might have mighty indwelling strength and strong encouragement to grasp and hold fast the hope appointed for us.... [Now] we have this [hope] as a sure and steadfast anchor of the soul... (See Hebrews 6:13-14, 17-19, AMB).

The fact that God has sworn to give you the blessings of Abraham should be an anchor to your soul! You should hold fast to it. When the devil comes to you and says you will not make it. You will never prosper. You will never have a good job. You never have that home you need...; God's promise and oath ought to rise up within you. You ought to say, "I am an heir. I have inherited a promise that in blessing, God will bless me. And in multiplying, He will multiply me. I rebuke you, unbelief! Now get out of here devil, you are not going to get my inheritance!"

Faith Opens the Door, that is what the devil does not want you know. He tries to talk us out of our Covenant Citizenship benefits and inheritance. He does not have any inheritance of his own. He has to steal everything he gets from the seed of Abraham, because the whole world belongs to us a Christians. We must be knowledgeable of our benefits and inheritance and this is gained through reading and studying of God's Word.

We must believe that what we are reading and studying is being revealed unto us to enjoy here and now and not to be put off until we get to Heaven. We must know and understand the means by which we can access the Covenant Citizenship benefits and inheritance that rightly belongs to us.

Summary

In order to receive your inheritance, *First* of all you must be in the family, *Second* you must be knowledgeable of your Covenant Citizenship benefits and your inheritance. *Third* you must live by faith. *Fourth* you cannot look at things from a natural perspective. You must leave the realm of the senses; (there is nothing in your senses that can connect you to the realm of the Spirit) where we receive from God in term of the things you desire. You must leave the realm of what you can taste, touch, see, feel, smell, and hear. Your senses, they have nothing to do with your receiving your inheritance. As you go forth in God claiming your Covenant Citizenship benefits and receiving your inheritance you have to act by faith. You are no longer able to look to your senses to see if something feels good, bad or indifferent. Whether you have it or not, your senses are not involved. (See Romans 4:13, 16-17, Galatians 5:29)

The natural sense belongs to the natural man; you are not the natural man once Christ comes to live within you. You are a spiritual man going after your Covenant Citizenship benefits and receiving your inheritance. But you act by faith. Once you get into the realm of faith, this is when you can obtain your inheritance, this is a realm where satan cannot get to because this is the eternal realm and satan is bound to the realm of the common mere man, and he must operate within level of the senses, and that is why he is called the god of This world.

That means he is the god of the senses. The devil will try to make you feel something that is not even true; we must ignore that and go by the Word of God. Now do you see why we that the true Kingdom citizens, born-again believers are register overcomers, unstoppable, invincible, and indestructible church of the living God! (See Joel 2:1-2)

Law of Faith

Purpose

The law of faith is safe and dependable. Faith is the law of God and it pleases God when we abide by that law. Faith is based upon the word of God and not what can be seen with the human eye. Operating in the law of faith requires us to know the word of God, a heart that believes in God's word, and a mouth that speaks God's word.

According to the Webster's dictionary, the meaning of the word law is, a principle based on the predictable consequences of an act, condition, etc.

Example of other laws:

The law of Faith is like God's law of gravity. It works. Believe it or not, it still works. The law of gravity works all the time. God's law of faith works all the time, as it's God's Law of Attraction! Electricity has laws, and there are also laws of aerodynamics. If you operate within the laws of electricity or aero dynamics, it is safe, performs well and is dependable. However if you break these laws, they can kill you.

Likewise, if you operate within the law of faith, it too, will be safe, it will perform for you, and it will be something to depend on. The problem is that some people don't "work it." The law of gravity is mandatory. The law of faith is optional. But God tells us how to operate in faith.

It will work whenever it is applied properly. Faith will not work if we fail to apply it according to God's specified way.

Faith is a law in the sense that electricity has laws, and there are also laws of aerodynamics. If you operate within the laws of electricity or aerodynamics, it is safe, performs well and is dependable. However if you break those laws, it can kill you. Likewise, if you operate within the law of faith, it too, will be safe, perform for you, and will be something to depend on.

Romans 3:23-27 "For all have sinned, and come short of the glory of God, [24]: Being justified freely by His grace through the redemption that is in Christ Jesus: [25]: Whom God hath set forth to be a propitiation through faith in His blood, to declare His righteousness for the remission of sins that are past, through the forbearance of God [26]: To declare I say, at this time His righteousness: that he might be just, and the justifier of him which believeth in Jesus, [27]: Where is boasting then? It is excluded, by what law? of works? Nay: but by the **law of faith**.

All of mankind has faith

For I say, through the grace given unto me, to every man that is among you, not to think of himself more highly than he ought to think; but to think soberly, according as God hath dealt to every man the measure of faith. (See Romans 12:3) Mankind has a free will to place it in, and exercise it on, whatever he wants.

In fact, man is a creature of faith. That is to say that he was created to live by faith. Man is driven by something in him to place his faith, (like an anchor), in something or someone in the desire to feel safe, sound and whole.

It really becomes a matter of just what his faith is in, as to what result will come of it. For example his faith may be in his education, his money, his strength, his doctor, his lawyer, his preacher, and on and on.

Faith is the Law of God

Hebrew 11:1 "Faith is the substance of things hoped for and the evidence of things not seen"

We please God when we operate in Faith.

Hebrew 11:6 "But without faith it is impossible to please Him: for that who comes to God must believe that He is, and that He is a rewarder of those who them that diligently seek him."

We believe that the carnal mind cannot operate in GOD'S LAW OF FAITH.

Romans 3:27; "Where is boasting then? It is excluded, by what law? of works? Nay: but by the law of faith." There are other laws like this, for instance, the law of the Spirit of life and the law of sin and death"

Romans 8:1-2; "There is therefore now no condemnation to them which are in Christ Jesus, who walk not after the flesh, but after the Spirit, For the law of the Spirit of life in Christ Jesus hath made me free from the law of sin and death."

Romans 12:3; "For l say, through the grace given unto me, to every man that is among you, not to think of himself more highly than he ought to think; but to think soberly, according as God hath dealt to every man the measure of faith."

James 1:5-7; "If any of you lack wisdom, let him ask of God, that giveth to all men liberally, and upbraideth not; and it shall be given him. ⁶But let him ask in faith, nothing wavering.

For he that wavereth is like a wave of the sea driven with the wind and tossed. ⁷ For let not that man think that he shall receive any thing of the Lord."

It also states in James that we have to be doers of the Word of God....not just hearers. We have to put our faith to work. Speak it, believe it without doubt!

We find the following in the book of James says ...

James1:23-24; "For if any be a hearer of the word, and not a doer, he is like unto a man beholding his natural face in a glass: ²⁴ For he beholdeth himself, and goeth his way, and straightway forgetteth what manner of man he was."

Faith Obeys the Word! - You have heard the adage "seeing is believing" well, that's not really true. The Bible indicates that "Believing is seeing through the eyes of Faith."(2 Corinthians 4:18).

True Faith is never blind. Faith always knows. Faith always sees. Faith is able to look through the storm and see the end results. Faith will always talk the end results, instead of what exists at present. Faith is acting of the Word of God!

The key to Understanding the Workings of Faith is in Mark 11:22-24; "But shall BELIEVE that those things which he SAYS shall come to pass; he shall have whatsoever, (Anything in line with the Word of God), he SAYS In verse twenty four;" therefore I say unto you, what things so-ever ye desire, when ye pray, believe that ye receive them, (Prior to their manifestation), and ye shall have them. (Emphasis added)"

You have to SPEAK His Words concerning healing. **You are SPEAKING them to:**

1. Confess (affirm) to God
2. Proclaim to the devil and
3. Confirm to yourself that you BELIEVE what you are saying.

In James 2:17; The Word of God tells us, "Even so faith, if it hath not works, is dead, being alone."

You must ACT on your faith for it to be released and produce anything! The withered hand had to be stretched out before it was made whole.

In Matthew 12:9-13; says… "⁹And when he was departed thence, he went into their synagogue: ¹⁰And, behold, there was a man which had his hand withered. And they asked him, saying, Is it lawful to heal on the Sabbath days? that they might accuse him, ¹¹And he said unto them, What man shall there be among you, that shall have one sheep, and if it fall into a pit on the sabbath day, will he not lay hold on it, and lift it out? ¹²How much then is a man better than a sheep? Wherefore it is lawful to do well on the Sabbath days. ¹³Then saith he to the man, Stretch forth thine hand. And he stretched it forth; and it was restored whole, like as the other."

We need to DO something that we could not previously do. Our faith has to be based on the written Word of God, whether it is for healing or anything else!

Faith, the Operation of God

Faith is acting on the WORD. It is not on your sensory mechanism, some philosophical reasoning, nor on theological concepts, but it's acting on God's Word.

Romans 10:9-10 NTL "If you confess with your mouth that Jesus is Lord and believe in your heart that God raised him from the dead, you will be saved. For it is by believing in your heart that you are made right with God, and it is by confessing with your mouth that you are saved."

Romans 3:27 "²⁷Where is boasting then? It is excluded By what law? Of works? Nay: but by the law of faith."

In order to participate in the operation of faith you must have three things:

1. You must have the Word of God (Logos\Rhema)
2. A Heart that believes the Word of God (1 Peter 3:4)
3. A Mouth that speaks (confesses) the Word of God
(Proverb 18:21)

Some scriptures are given to show what the Word of God is teaching us the secret of faith is to be a co-labor with the Spirit of God, it is necessary to know what the ground rules are so that we can operate in faith.

Listed below some examples of the Operations of Faith:

1. God said, "Let there be" Genesis 1:3-25;
2. Abraham "Father of many nations" Genesis 17:3-40
3. Conquest of Jericho: Joshua 6:16 -20;
4. Naaman, the Syria healed: 2 King 5:1-4, 8-14;
5. Peter acting on the Word of God. Luke 5:1-9;

The simplest way to the operation of faith is to learn to believe the Word and act on it. You don't know if you are really a believer until you are willing to demonstrate your belief.

It is through acting on the Word of God that you move from believing to faith. James chapter one and verse twenty two; states that, "We are not to be hearers only, but doers of the Word of God."

The operation of faith calls those things, which be not as though they were. Instead of them being based upon what you see; they are based upon the Word of God. The universe, in which live, contains many laws. Again everyone is very familiar with is the law of gravity. Everyone knows what goes up must come down.

The law, by which we access the things of God, is called the Law of Faith. The Law of Faith operates when we learn to "Call those things which be not as though they were", (2 Corinthians 4:18). We can apply this law, because we are born-again.

2 Corinthians 4:13; "We having the same spirit of faith, according as it is written, I believed, and therefore have I spoken; we also believe, and therefore speak"

There are many who operate in faith from a negative prospective. Listed below are some examples of negative phrases that people use without realizing it.

1. "My feet are killing me." (1 Peter 2:24)
2. "I am scared to death." (2 Timothy 1:7)
3. "I am confused." (1 Corinthians 14:30)
4. "I am broke, busted, and can't be trusted" (Phil. 4:19)
5. "Well if it's not one things it is another" (Mark 11:23)
6. "I am so weak" (Joel 3:10b)
7. "Girl I am about to lose my mind" (1Corinthians. 2:16)

We, as believers, have the ability of operate in faith without an understanding the workings of faith. It is the enemy who is influencing us to use such phrases because he knows that it is detrimental to our lives. By understanding the proper working of faith, we can receive the wonderful blessings of God.

Romans 5:1-3; "Therefore being justified by faith, we have peace with God through Our Lord Jesus Christ: By whom also we have access by faith into this grace wherein we stand, and rejoice in hope of the glory of God and not only so, but we glory in tribulations also: knowing that tribulation worketh patience;"

As believers, we have the God kind of faith and must act according to

Mark 11:22-24; "22And Jesus answering saith unto them, Have faith in God. 23For verily I say unto you, That whosoever shall say unto this mountain, Be thou removed, and be thou cast into the sea; and shall not doubt in his heart, but shall believe that those things which he saith shall come to pass; he shall have whatsoever he saith. 24Therefore I say unto you, what things soever ye desire, when ye pray, believe that ye receive them, and ye shall have them."

I trust that you have seen from the biblical examples how the operations of the God kind of faith, works. In order to be successful in the things of God, it is necessary to know what the ground rules are, so that we can be co-laborers with the Spirit of God. It is through faith that we have access to the wonderful blessings that He has for us to enjoy while on earth.

Summary

Faith is trusting in God and not man. For man has the ability to fail, whereas, God never fails. When you walk by faith, there is no room for doubts. When you walk by faith, there is no time for worries. When you walk by faith, mountains will be moved. Always know God's word, have a believing heart and confess with your mouth God's word. According to Hebrews 11:6, it states that without faith it is impossible to please God, but as we Yoke up with Jesus and the Kingdom and the Law of faith we will always be in faith, thus always pleasing our Heavenly Father.

The Law of Confession

Proverbs 18:21; "Death and life *are* in the power of the tongue: and they that love it shall eat the fruit thereof."

There is power in the words that we speak. We reap what we sow and words are seeds. Therefore, if the words we speak are negative, than we reap negativity. And, if we speak words that are positive, than we reap positivity.

Everything that's happening in your life right now; being good or bad is the result of words. Not just your words. It could be words from family members, friends, teachers, etc. Even if there are undesirable situations you are dealing with; just remember that words can also turn situations around.

The Power of Words - The universe we live in functions based upon laws and principles; such as the law of attraction, the law of gravity, and etc. God created the universe to function that way. Jesus said... I will give you the keys to the kingdom (Matthew 16:19)

One way to operate this law in Yoking up with Jesus is learning the value of Words, especially the Word of God. Many Christians don't understand the law of Confession. One way a couple becomes one is by saying the same thing. So one way of Yoking up with Jesus is by valuing and speak only what thus saith the Lord, the Word of God.

In Matthew 13:17-19 Jesus says

"…¹⁷For verily I say unto you, that many prophets and righteous men have desired to see those things which ye see, and have not seen them; and to hear those things which ye hear, and have not heard them. ¹⁸Hear ye therefore the parable of the sower ¹⁹When any one heareth the word of the kingdom, and understandeth it not, then cometh the wicked one, and catcheth away that which was sown in his heart. This is he which received seed by the way side God created this universe with the words that He spoke and likewise, you were made to manifest every word that you speak. There is power in your words and you will have what you say whether it is good or bad…so watch your mouth.

For Example, in the book of Daniel, Nebuchadnezzar, King of Babylon, had made a law that everyone must fall down and worship the golden statue when the music starting playing. There were three Hebrews who were among the Jews in Babylonian captivity, who were defiant saying in Daniel 3:18, "… "We will not serve thy gods nor worship the golden image which thou has set up".

They were refusing to serve the gods of the Babylonians because it conflicted with the law of their God Jehovah which said, in Exodus 20:2-5 "…"Thou shall have no other gods before me… thou shall not bow down thyself to them, nor serve them" Thus, the three Hebrews in refusing to bow, chose to live by the Word of God in their hearts rather than the written laws of a heathen nation.

They believed and decreed their deliverance saying, "...Our God whom we serve is able to deliver us from the burning fiery furnace, and He will deliver us out of thy hand, O king." And, as it was expected, He did. Supernaturally! They were living by the Word of God in their hearts instead of an external system.

Now you can understand what David wrote, Psalm 119:11 says "...Thy word have I hid in my heart, that I might not sin against thee" Another example of this "Kingdom living," or living from the inside out, is found in the New Testament, in the Gospel according to Mark 4:35-41.

Notice what Jesus used to stop the storm? In Matthew 12:34; He released words. Where did these words come from? From the Father and were stored in His Heart. "Out of the abundance of the heart the mouth speaketh. Oh, He could do that because He was God in the flesh." That's true, but Jesus sat His Godhead abilities aside and functioned in this earth as a man anointed by God. Paul called Him the last Adam. They said, "What manner of man is this that even the wind and the sea obey Him."

In the book of Proverbs it tells us that, "Death and life are in the power of the tongue: and they that love it shall eat the fruit thereof. Notice what it didn't say. It didn't say death and life are in the power of the devil. Neither did it say in the power of God. No, It said, "Death and life are in the power of the tongue," that includes "your tongue." Jesus, being controlled by the Word of God on the inside of Him, spoke life to this situation.

The disciple, on the other hand, under pressure of the raging storm spoke death saying, "... We're all about to drown."

How many of us believers have done this same thing? We have operated under the control of external circumstances and not by God's Word. Remember, words are seeds in the spirit realm. And, they are programmed to produce a harvest of whatever is sown. You may have something in your life that you want to be rid of. It might be poverty, failures, sickness, or a feeling of inferiority.

Whatever it is that you have in your life are harvests or the manifestation of seeds that have been sown. Nothing just happens. It could be your words, words of your parents, your teachers, your close friends, or words sown into your grandmother and passed on to you in the form of how you were trained. The bottom line is, where you are now is the result of somebody's words.

Speak the Words only! - In the book of Proverbs 18:21 it tells us that, "Death and life are in the power of the tongue: and they that love it shall eat the fruit thereof"

In Proverbs 26:22 the words of a talebearer are as wounds, and they go down into the innermost parts of the belly. Let us examine this principle a bit closer. Every word we speak is a seed and if conceived or planted in the soil of the heart (spirit) will bring forth a harvest"... after his kind" (Genesis 1:11) From the beginning, starting with Adam and Eve, God never intended for mankind to speak anything he or she didn't want or believe that it would come to pass.

I read where a man said that God told him, "instead of my people having what they say, they are saying what they have".

Proverbs 6:2; "Thou art snared with the words of thy mouth; thou art taken with the words of thy mouth"

Proverbs 10:19; "In the multitude of words there wanteth not sin: but he that refraineth his lips is wise."

I read another statement where a man who needed surgery. He kept saying to his relatives and to the physician, "if I have to undergo an operation, I know I'll die."

Guess what? The doctor refused to operate. He knew the power of words.

Joel said..."*Let the weak say, I am strong*" (Joel 3:10).

2 Corinthians 4:18; "While we look not at the things which are seen, but at the things which are not seen: for the things which are seen are temporal; but the things which are not seen are eternal."

Romans 4:17; "As it is written, I have made thee a father of many nations, before him whom he believed, even God, who quickeneth the dead, and calleth those things which be not as though they were."

God created this universe with the words that He spoke and likewise, you were made to manifest every word that you speak. There is power in your words and you will have what you say whether it is good or bad...so watch your mouth.

Jesus came preaching the Kingdom of God. He was reintroducing the Kingdom of God to man, bringing us back up to where mankind was before the fall, ruling this earth with words.

I call it Kingdom Living, "Kingdom living" is simply living by the Word of God in our hearts rather than under the control of an external system or circumstance.

Three examples that will explain the law of confession: The law of Confession means to speak the same thing that God says:

Jesus said ..." For verily I say unto you, that whosoever shall say unto this mountain, be thou removed, and be thou cast into the sea; and shall not doubt in his heart, but shall believe that those things which he saith shall come to pass; he shall have whatsoever he saith. (Mark 11:23)

Jesus said unto him, "if thou canst believe, all things are possible to him that believeth." (Mark 9:23)

In order to show you exactly how law of Confession works we are given examples within the scriptures:

James 3:2, 3 "²For in many things we offend all. If any man offend not in word, the same is a perfect man, and able also to bridle the whole body. ³Behold, we put bits in the horses' mouths that they may obey us; and we turn about their whole body.

The way that mankind has tamed and controlled horses is by placing a bit in their mouths; The way that the riders is able to control, and have the horse to go in the direction that he or she desires to go is by applying pressure on the tongue of the horse. When you desire for the horse to turn right you pull on the side of the bit. But, perhaps you didn't know this and just thought that it was just pulling against the horses' jaw. No, when you pull on the bit you are actually putting pressure on the horses' tongue.

It is the tongue that causes the whole body to turn. Initially when the bit is placed in the horses' mouth, it will show some resistance to the pressure but as the rider continue to apply the pressure you will notice that the whole body becomes subject to that pressure and began to cooperate with the rider.

Another illustration is found in

James 3:4 says… "4Behold also the ships, which though they be so great, and are driven of fierce winds, yet are they turned about with a very small helm, whithersoever the governor listeth."

I don't know about you, but I have seen some cruise ships and they are pretty big, and when the Captain needs to turn the ship in a certain direction he doesn't jump into the water and turn the ship in the direction that he wasn't it to go. There is a steering wheel at the front of the ship. The entire steering apparatus of a ships' steering wheel is attached to a rudder (fore-and-after line) that causes the ship to turn the number of degrees by applying pressure to the rubber.

James 3:5-6 says…"5Even so the tongue is a little member, and boasteth great things. Behold how great a matter a little fire kindleth! 6And the tongue is a fire, a world of iniquity: so is the tongue among our members, that it defileth the whole body, and setteth on fire the course of nature; and it is set on fire of hell."

I remember when I was a young child my dad would get up early in the morning and start a fire in a pot belly stove. When we got up it was nice and warm. When my dad got up very early in the morning the house would be extremely cold and after the fire get going the house would began to get comfortable. Once my brother and I got older we were responsible for getting kindling and wood for our heating system back then.

My brother and I would go down in the woods and look for wood that was very dry and wood that had sap on it. Sap is a syrupy type substance and great for starting a fire, because once the kindling was lit and burning it would cause the other wood to catch afire. The kindling was the little member in the stove, but once it got started it would cause everything to catch a fire.

Think about all of the problems or issues that you have had in life, It has been because of your tongue or somebody else tongue.

Proverbs 18:8 and 26:22 says." The words of a talebearer are as wounds, and they go down into the innermost parts of the belly."

You may have something in your life that you want to be rid of. It might be poverty, failure, sickness, or a feeling of inferiority. Whatever it is in your life; good or bad, are harvests or the manifestation of seeds that have been sown.

Again, everything happens for a reason. It could be your words, words of your parents, your teachers, your close friends, or words sown into your grandmother and passed on to you in the form of how you were trained. The bottom line is, where you are now is the result of somebody's words. There are no situations that you can't turn around with words.

The Mystery of Confession - Spiritual Law - God and His creation operate according to spiritual laws. These laws cannot be violated and when properly used these spiritual laws will always produce the desired results.

Example of Confession:

"In Christ I am anointed and a powerful person of God. I am a joint-heir with Jesus and more than a conqueror. I am a doer of the Word of God and a channel for His blessings, if God be for me, who can be against me?"

"We must understand that there are laws governing every single thing in existence. Nothing is by accident. There are laws of the world of the spirit, and there are laws of the world of the natural. We need to realize that the spiritual world and its laws are more powerful than the physical world and its laws. Spiritual laws gave birth to physical laws . . . God a Spirit, created all matters . . . with the force of faith.

Positive Confession - God creates by confessing what He wants. We are created in His image, thus we too have the ability to release faith-filled words and thus create what we need in life. Spiritual law generally works by confessing properly what you need. If you need physical healing you confess passages of text on prosperity.

The "spiritual law" is simple

(1) Believe in your heart,
(2) Confess it with your mouth, and
(3) Believe you have it and you will see the manifestation of it "What you are believe that you receive" (Mark 11:23-24).

"Even though God had the image inside Him and the Spirit of God was there to cause it to come to pass, it had to be released out of His mouth before any changes could take place. God used His words to bring the image into manifestation. He filled His words with the spiritual force of faith."

The High Priest of Our Confession

Very few believers today understand the mystery of the Apostleship and Priesthood of Jesus. We think that an apostle is some kind of super saint. But "apostle" actually means, "Sent one." So, Jesus has been sent from God to do something for us. He's been sent to serve as our High Priest.

Again, many believers don't have the first idea what a high priest does. They picture a person walking around in strange clothes performing religious rituals.

In reality, a high priest is much more than that. He is one who is authorized to administer, to execute, or to carry out on your behalf.

Hebrews 3:1; "Wherefore, holy brethren, partakers of the heavenly calling, consider the Apostle and High Priest of our profession, Christ Jesus;" He's been sent to put into effect, to carry out the words that you say. (Isaiah 55:8-11, Psalm 103:20, Hebrews 1:14)

Question - Have you been speaking what you feel, instead of speaking words of faith? If, for example, you're speaking sickness, what's He going do with that? He's not High Priest over sickness.

He can't execute that. If you're saying, "I'm so weak, I'm so tired," He can't carry that out. The Bible says, "Let the weak say, I am strong!" The minute you say that, Jesus can administer STRENGTH.

Jesus is not going to administer sickness or disease or poverty or sin. He's defeated all that. He is High Priest over deliverance and righteousness and freedom. Consider that, and then as you come before Jesus, don't speak words of defeat. Speak words He can implement words of victory. That's what He's been ordained by God to bring to pass in your life. Many people fail to receive what they pray for because of lack of understanding about confession.

Again in Hebrews 3:1 we are commanded to "consider Christ Jesus the Apostle and High Priest of our confession." As our High Priest Jesus acts in our behalf according to what we confess when it is in accordance with God's Word.

The devil knows! - In Genesis 3:1-7 now the serpent was craftier than any of the wild animals the LORD God had made. He said to the woman, "Did God really say, 'You must not eat from any tree in the garden'?" The woman said to the serpent, "We may eat fruit from the trees in the garden, but God did say, 'You must not eat fruit from the tree that is in the middle of the garden, and you must not touch it, or you will die.'

"You will not surely die," the serpent said to the woman. "God knows that when you eat of it your eyes will be opened, and you will be like God, knowing good and evil."

When the woman saw that the fruit of the tree was good for food and pleasing to the eye, and also desirable for gaining wisdom, she took some and ate it. She also gave some to her husband, who was with her, and he ate it. Then the eyes of both of them were opened, and they realized they were naked; so they sewed fig leaves together and made coverings for themselves.

Additional Examples: – Jacob / Rachel Genesis 31:30-32 and 35:17- 19; Gabriel / Zachariah – Luke 1:1 -24;

What happened? The fall of Man; it is important for us to understand how the devil tricked Adam and Eve into disobeying God. Military intelligence of enemy tactics is crucial in a war. We are in a spiritual war until Jesus comes back. Therefore, we must understand the tactics of the enemy if we are to be successful in daily battles. Paul taught us that we should not be unaware of the devil's tactics in 2 Corinthians 2:11. With that in mind, let's take a closer look at his tactics:

Changing God's Word - The first thing that the enemy did was to cast doubt on what God said. He attacked God's command and attempted to twist God's Words. This is why it is so very important for us to know and understand the Word of God for ourselves. (Matthew 13:28-31). The bible speaks of false prophets coming to lead many astray. Most people are led astray, like Eve was, because they allow someone to come and confuse them about the Word of God.

We need to clearly understand the Word of God and how it applies to our daily lives. The father or Lies: John taught us that the devil is a liar and the father of it (John 8:44). He uses lies to deceive people daily.

In the text, he told Eve that:

(1) She would not die and that,

(2) If she ate of the fruit, her eyes would be opened and she would, be like God. The problem here is that God told Eve she would die (spiritually). Furthermore, she was already like God.

(3) We must learn why man was created? Man in His image and likeness and gave man dominion in the earth. Man was already like God and this act would actually cause the separation between God and man.

The Big Three: Towards the end of the book, John teaches us to stay away from what I call 'The Big Three.' He said, (1 John 2:16) For all that is in the world, the lust of the flesh, and the lust of the eyes, and the pride of life, is not of the Father, but is of the world.

We now go back to the beginning of the book and find the same three tactics. The text says when the woman saw that the fruit of the tree was good for food (the lust of the flesh) and pleasing to the eye (the lust of the eyes), and also desirable for gaining wisdom (the pride of life), she took some and ate it.

Summary

These are the same three tactics that the devil uses against us daily and the sad part is that we keep falling for them.

- We need to know the Word of God and not allow anyone to twist God's Word and lead us astray.

- We must recognize that the devil is the father of lies and realize that he will consistently attack us through lying.

- We must understand the 'Big Three' tactics of the devil and make every attempt not to allow ourselves to be caught by them.

Daily Favor Confession

In the name of Jesus, I am the righteousness of God. Therefore, I am entitled to covenant kindness and covenant favor. The favor of God is among the righteous. The favor of God surrounds the righteous. Therefore, it surrounds me everywhere I go and in everything I do. I expect the favor of God to be in full manifestation in my life. Never again will I be without the favor of God. It rests richly upon me. It profusely abounds in me.

I am a part of the generation that is experiencing God's favor immeasurably, limitlessly and surpassingly. Therefore, favor produces supernatural increase, promotion, restoration, honor, increased assets, greater victories, recognition, prominence, preferential treatment, petitions granted (prayers answered), policies and rules changed, and battles won in which I do not have to fight! The favor of God is on me and goes before me. Therefore, my life will never be the same! This is the year of God's favor in my life. That is the favor of God, In Jesus' name. Amen.

Scripture References: II Corinthians 9:8, Exodus 12:35-36, Genesis 39:21, Luke 2:52, Deuteronomy 33:23, Esther 8:5, Esther 5:8, Psalms 44:3, Psalms 102:13

MAKEAKE FAITH DECLARATIONS; WHO I AM, WHAT I HAVE, AND WHAT I CAN DO!

MONDAY - I WALK IN LOVE AND FAITH

- **Jesus is Lord** over my spirit, my soul, and my body;
- I Thank You Heavenly Father that your love has been shed abroad in my heart by the Holy Spirit and that your love abides in me richly;
- Heavenly Father, I Love You, with all my heart, with all my soul, with all my strength, and with all my money-might;
- I Love my neighbor as myself.
- Heavenly Father, I thank you, that I am filled with YOUR fullness.
- I am rooted and grounded in Love;
- I keep myself in the Kingdom of light, in Love, in the Word, and the wicked one touches me not;
- I am a spirit, I have a soul, I live in a physical body;
- I am in the world, but I am not of this world;
- I am born of the Spirit, and filled with the Spirit of God, and I am led by the Spirit of God;
- I trust in the Lord, with all of my heart and I lean not to my own understanding;
- In all my ways I acknowledge Him, and He directs my paths. My pathway is life and not death;
- I walk in the light of the Word of God;
- Heavenly Father, Your WORD is lamp unto my feet;
- Heavenly Father, Your WORD is a light unto my path;
- Heavenly Father, your WORD is food unto my spirit;
- Heavenly Father, Your Word shall not depart out of my mouth. I meditate therein day and night;
- I shall make way prosperous;

- I will have good success in life;
- I am a doer of Your Word and put Your Word first;
- I center everything around the WORD of God;
- I am a believer and not a doubter;
- I hold fast to my confession of faith;
- I decide to walk by faith and practice faith;
- My faith comes by hearing and hearing by the Word of God;
- Jesus is the author and the developer of my faith;
- I take my shield of faith and quench every fiery dart that the wicked one brings against me;
- I am the just, I live by faith, I please my Heavenly Father.

TUESDAY - I FLOW IN THE GUIDANCE OF THE HOLY SPIRIT

- **Heavenly Father**, Please don't Let me miss you today, use me every day in a mighty way. Let me sense your presence and your fresh renewal every day of my life;
- I thank you for the memories of yesterday, but I need to experience you today, I am expecting great things from you tomorrow. Yesterday is gone, but today and tomorrow I live in expectation of a new and wonderful outpouring of your Mighty Spirit in my life;
- I am born of the Spirit, filled with the Spirit of God;
- The Holy Spirit dwells within me;
- The Spirit of truth abideth in me and teaches me all things and guides me into all truths;
- I am what Word of God says I am;
- I can do what the Word of God says I can do;
- I have what the Word of God says I have;
- I am a spirit, I have a soul, and I live in a physical body;
- I am in the world, but I am not of this world;
- I am made in God's image;
- I have God's nature on the inside of me;
- I have God's ability within me through Christ;
- I am working together with Christ;
- Gods plan is for me to go forth in His ability and power;
- I am bold, I am courageous, I am a strong person;
- God is my Father, He is for me, who can be against me;
- Holy Spirit, You are my counselor; Teaching me, educating me, training me, and develop my human spirit;
- Greater is He that is in me than he that is in the world;
- The Holy Spirit dwells within me.

WEDNESDAY - I WALK IN THE MIRACLE WORKING POWER OF GOD

- **Heavenly Father**, Thank You for Your mercy and grace.
- I am born-again; I am filled with the Holy Spirit.
- I am a supernatural being, filled with the supernatural power of God;
- I am made in the image of God;
- Through the Holy Spirit within me, I have the same miracle-working power that Christ has, to do the same mighty works He did;
- I am a believer and I am expecting His miracle power to be released within me to meet the desperate needs of those around me;
- Thank you that you are releasing your miracle power and other are being minister unto in spirit, soul and body by your Spirit and through your WORD.

THURSDAY - I AM HEALED

- **Heavenly Father,** I bless you and I love you;
- I bless and love my enemies;
- I forgive them now and I release them in the name of Jesus;
- Christ has redeemed from every sickness written in the curse of the law;
- I am redeemed from every disease that is not written in the book of the law;
- Christ has redeemed me, brought me back and set me FREE from all sickness and diseases;
- I have been delivered from the authority of darkness;
- In Christ Jesus I have redemption;
- I have been ransom from captivity;
- I am delivered from satan dominion and his work;
- I am free from sickness and disease;
- I am healed;
- I am a member of the Body of Christ;
- I am redeemed from the curse, because Jesus bore my sickness and carried my diseases in His own body. By His stripes I am healed;
- I forbid any sickness or disease to operate in my body;
- Every organ, every tissue of my body functions in the perfection in which God created it to function;
- I honor God and bring glory to Him in my body.

FRIDAY - ALL MY MATERIAL AND FINANCIAL NEEDS ARE PROVIDED

- Jesus has destroyed the curse over my life;
- Christ has redeemed me from the curse of the law;
- For poverty He has given me wealth;
- I am prosperous, rich, and wealthy;
- I am out of debt and all my needs are met;
- I have plenty more to put in store;
- I sow bountifully; I reap bountifully;
- I am attracting your blessing like a magnet;
- I am full of Joy, full of life;
- I am Healed, I am Debt free;
- Lord I acknowledge you this day;
- You have sent your angels unto me to walk with me;
- Angels walk in front of me to prepare my way; they walk behind me to protect me from area that I cannot see;
- Angels walk beside me for comfort and company;
- Angels are with me today;
- Where ever I go is prosperous;
- I am prosperous in every area of my life;
- Everything I put my hands to prosper;
- The world must make way for me; because (**Your Name**) in the Lord Jesus Christ, as an ambassador of the Kingdom of God is coming through; Fear not, God is my shield, Abundant compensation, and my reward shall be exceedingly great! I will never worry about where my next meal is going to come from, or the next meal for my family; My kitchen cabinets, refrigerators, and freezers are full; I have all the resource that is necessary to live a life fill with abundance.

SATURDAY - TO WALK IN THE FAVOR AND WISDOM OF GOD

- **Heavenly Father,** I thank you because you are doing exceedingly abundantly above all that I can ask or Think Your mighty power is taking over in me;
- I am an heir of God through Jesus Christ;
- I am a joint-heir with Jesus Christ;
- I let the word of God dwell in me richly;
- He who began a good work in me will continue until the day of Christ;
- I have perfect knowledge of every situation and every circumstance that I come up against. Jesus has been made unto me wisdom, righteousness, sanctification, and redemption;
- I have the wisdom of God,
- I am the righteousness of God in Christ Jesus;
- I am sanctified and sealed by the Holy Spirit;
- I am the redeemed of the Lord;
- I have an abundance, Favor flowing from God to me
- I am a success today, I have God's special favor me
- I think like it, live like it, drive like it, dress like it;
- I am expecting great things to happen in my life;
- I obtained favor in the sight of all
- I will meet nice people today;
- I shall have good relationships with people today;
- I shall favor and honor others today;
- I am a blessing to the Lord. I am a blessing to others;
- Lord Jesus, You are my Lord and my Savior.

SUNDAY - I WALK IN THE BLESSING

- **Heaven Father**, I Thank You that I am blessed because I am born into BLESSING;
- Thank you that the blessing is working in me, on me, and around me;
- I declare that I am blessed when I come in and I am blessed when I go out;
- Jesus came to the earth to restore the blessing that Adam lost in the Garden of Eden when he sinned;
- I am a child of God. I have a covenant right to the blessing;
- I declare that like Abraham I am blessed to be a blessing until all the families of the earth are blessed, the blessing of God is on my life;
- I am empowered to prosper in every endeavor that I take on and every project that I begin;
- I am blessed on my job;
- I am blessed in all my relationships. Like Joseph, those in authority over me see the blessing of God on my life;
- I have favor as a result. Thanks for blessing me with all spiritual blessings in heavenly places;
- I am powerful, wealthy, influential and blessed! In Jesus Name Amen.

A Special Note to the Reader!

Before reading this book, perhaps you were a citizen of His Kingdom living beneath your means and rightful status, being unaware of your benefits. Or perhaps you were a Kingdom citizen who knows about the benefits, but lacked the motivation to operate on your knowledge and stake a claim to what is rightfully yours.

It is my prayer that after learning about the rights, privileges and promises to which you are entitled that are contained in this booklet; you now have the desire to act upon this information to bring about a change in your life.

Remember, receiving your Kingdom benefits is a three-fold process: you have the information; now, make your requests (Petition) known unto God, Your Father and when you receive what you have requested of Him, apply what He gives you and maximize it in your life!

He has given us, as His children, these covenant citizenship benefits and Inheritances to help us live a victorious life. Let us bless the heart of our Heavenly Father by receiving them and applying them to our lives as He intended.

Are you ready to claim your Covenant benefits? Understanding and Claiming your Covenant Citizenship Inheritance If yes, on the next few Pages there is a list of scriptures to help you to <u>establish</u> a relationship with the God and become a citizen of the Kingdom through receiving His only begotten Son Jesus who is the Christ.

Covenant Decision

As I have shared with you about the subject of claiming your covenant benefits and Inheritance, the only way that you can experience and walk in blessing of God covenant is by receiving the Lord Jesus Christ as your own personal Lord and Savior.

Jesus said "except you are born again yea shall not see the Kingdom of God" (John 3:3).

If you desire to experience the **Covenant benefits** that were covered in this booklet and in the Holy Bible, you must be born-again in order to qualify to be a partaker on the Covenant benefits. (Colossians 1:12)

Are you born again?

Listed are some scripture references that you can check out in the Bible to verify what we are saying. There is a short prayer that you can pray to receive the Lord Jesus Christ as your own personal Lord and Savior, and when you do that, You will be born into the Kingdom of God.

To receive Jesus Christ as your own personal Lord and Savior

Are you born again? Have you ever received Jesus as your Lord and Savior? If the answer to this question is no, read these scriptures and pray this prayer, agreeing with it and believing it from your heart

John 3:16 "For God so loved the world, that he gave his only begotten Son, that whosoever believeth in him should not perish, but have everlasting life"

Romans 10:9-10, 13 "That if thou shalt confess with thy mouth the Lord Jesus, and shalt believe in thine heart that God hath raised him from the dead, thou shalt be saved.

For with the heart man believeth unto righteousness; and with the mouth **Confession** is made unto salvation. For whosoever shall call upon the name of the Lord shall be saved.

John 14:6 " Jesus said unto him, I am the way, the truth and the life: no man cometh unto the Father, but by me."

PRAY THIS PRAYER

Dear Heavenly Father,
I come to you now and humbly ask for forgiveness. Lord I confess that I'm a sinner and I've broken your Holy law. I realize that the penalty of sin is death. I believe that Jesus Christ suffered and died on the cross to take the punishment for all my sins. I believe that Jesus rose from the dead and I accept Him as my personal Saviour, from this moment forward I give you my heart and trust you to be the Lord of my life. Please forgive all my sins and send Your Spirit to help me to do your will. I thank you for your great love and your gift of eternal life; I pray this in Jesus Name.

Signed _____

Date _____

About the Author

Pastor James L. Monteria is born again, and called to minister the Gospel of the Kingdom of Almighty God. Faith Christian Fellowship, International of Tulsa, Oklahoma, ordains him to execute the call on his life. He attended Rhema Bible Training Center of Broken Arrow a suburb of Tulsa, Oklahoma where he earned a Diploma in Ministerial Training.

Pastor Monteria received his Bachelor's of Science Degree in Business Administration from Saint Paul's College in Lawrenceville, VA. He received a Master's Degree in Instructional Education from Central Michigan University, Mount Pleasant, Michigan.

Pastor Monteria has ministered the Word of God through seminars, church services, Bible studies, Prison Ministries, distributions of his books, CD's and DVD's. Pastor Monteria believes that the Bible is the Word of God, and he is an anointed Pastor and Teacher of the Word of God.

His ministries are combination of anointed Preaching and Teaching the Word of God and flowing in the gifts of the Holy Spirit as He leads.

Pastor J. L. Monteria is available:

~Speaking Engagements~
~Book Signings~
~Workshops\Conferences~

You may contact J L Monteria via
Email address: comeandlearnofme@gmail.com
Mail address: P. O Box 932 Chesterfield, Va 23832
Products Website: www.clmpublication.info

www.ingramcontent.com/pod-product-compliance
Lightning Source LLC
Chambersburg PA
CBHW070814100426
42742CB00012B/2362